CHAKRAS

Ganesha Mantra

गजाननम् भूत गणादि सेवितम्
कपित्य्यजम्ब् फल चारु भक्षणम्
उमा सुतम् शोक विनाश कारकम्
नमामि विघ्नेश्वर पाद पंकजम्

CHAKRAS
Energy Centers of Transformation

HARISH JOHARI

Destiny Books
Rochester, Vermont

Destiny Books
One Park Street
Rochester, Vermont 05767
www.InnerTraditions.com

Destiny Books is a division of Inner Traditions International

Library of Congress Cataloging-in-Publication Data

Johari, Harish, 1934–1999.
    Chakras : energy centers of transformation / Harish Johari.—Newly rev.
  and enl. ed., Rev. and expanded ed.
        p. cm.
    Includes index.
    ISBN 978-089281760-3
    1. Chakra (Hinduism) 2. Kundalini 3. Yoga. I. Title.

  BL1215.C45 J64 2000
  294.5'436—dc21

                                                                00-043059

Printed and bound in India by Replika Press Pvt. Ltd.

10   9

Text design and layout by Priscilla H. Baker
This book was typeset in Bembo with Tiepolo and Stone Sans as the display typefaces

Contents

Acknowledgments

I would like to thank Pieter Weltevrede for preparing the line drawings and paintings for the first through sixth chakras for this revised edition, which were based on classical drawings and paintings of the chakras rendered by Sandeep Johari that appeared in the first edition of *Chakras*. I am very grateful to my teacher Shri C. Bal, who guided both Sandeep and Pieter in preparing these colored illustrations, and to Heidi Rauhut for preparing the first copy of the revised text of this new edition.

I am very thankful to H. H. Shripadji, Ganesh Baba, and Acharya Chandrashakhar Shastri for their clarification and guidance on various issues, and for enriching my knowledge by their teachings, blessings, and presence, which inspired me to undertake the job.

Finally, I thank all of my friends and students whose valuable suggestions have helped me prepare this book, and I hope that it in turn will be helpful as a guidebook to the chakras.

෪

Harish Johari left his body on August 20, 1999, at his home in the holy town of Haridwar. Pratibha Johari, family members, and Harish's students would like to thank the publisher, Ehud C. Sperling, for making it possible to continue Harish's work. Many thanks also to the editors, Jeanie Levitan and Nancy Yeilding, for their intensive collaboration on this edition.

Introduction

This book is an introduction to the classical understanding of chakras, which are most simply defined as psychic centers of transformation that enable one to move toward an enlightened state of being. Although the roots of the knowledge about chakras are of ancient origin, this knowledge is still functionally practical today. *Chakra* is a Sanskrit word that means "a wheel, a disc, or any arrangement in circular form or organization." The ancient sources depict each of the seven major chakras as a lotus blossom, a circular form surrounded by petals, as we shall see illustrated in chapter 3, "The Essentials of the Chakras." The word *chakra* also indicates movement. Chakras introduce movement because they transform psychophysical energy into spiritual energy.

Psychophysical energy is electrochemical in nature and it works with the help of *prana*. *Prana* is the energy that creates life, matter, and mind. The word *prana* means "vital life force." Although our organism draws *prana* in through our nostrils as we breathe, dynamic *prana* energy is not based on the physiochemical system of the body; it operates super-physically through a "wireless" system rather than through the nervous system.

Our body exists at two levels. The gross material level is composed of the seven *dhatus*—flesh, bone, clay, blood, fat, marrow, fluids—and the five elements—earth, water, fire, air, and *akasha* (the void or space). The subtle level is composed of the vital life force *(prana)*, mind *(manas)*, intellect *(buddhi)*, ego *(ahamkara)*, and the feeling self *(chitta)*. *Prana* is the means by which the subtle and the gross in the human organism are connected. It activates all of the systems in the body, including the nervous system, and helps them work together as they should.

Prana is distributed throughout the body by Nadis, channels of energy. The Nadi transport system belongs to the subtle body and the chakras are connected to the main Nadi of this system, the Sushumna, which operates within the vertebral (spinal) column. Chakras thus do not belong to the material body and cannot be described fully from a materialistic standpoint. Just as a painting cannot be described merely from the standpoint of its lines, curves, or varying shades of color, even though these can be said to form its basic structure, chakras cannot be defined physiologically, or through any physical science such as neurochemistry. However, chakras are not imaginary centers; they are subtle centers that can be activated by the techniques described in this book.

Chakras are active at all times, whether we are conscious of them or not. Energy influenced by the elements—earth, water, fire, air, and *akasha*—moves through the chakras, producing different psychic states. These elements *(tattvas)* are constantly moving with the breath inside the body and influencing one's temperament. (These changes are understood by neurobiologists as chemical changes produced by the endocrine glands, ductless glands whose secretions mix into the body's blood stream directly and instantaneously.) With training, it is possible to observe oneself and see energy moving through these various psychic centers. In chapter 3, "The Essentials of the Chakras," we will explain in detail the attributes and effects of the chakras. We also will explore the behavioral characteristics related to the chakras, which are not typically found in books on the subject.

There are seven major chakras, associated with the areas of the body and the elements as shown:

1. Muladhara Chakra: the base of the spine and the element earth

2. Svadhishthana Chakra: the genitals and the element water

3. Manipura Chakra: the navel and the element fire

4. Anahata Chakra: the heart and the element air

5. Vishuddha Chakra: the throat and the element *akasha* (void or space)

6. Ajna Chakra: the point between the eyebrows and *mahatattva*, the combination of the essence of all the elements in their purest form

7. Sahasrara Chakra: the crown of the head, transcending all elemental influence; includes the Soma Chakra, associated with the area above the "third eye" or point between the eyebrows

Knowledge about the chakras as psychic centers can be a valuable key to introspection. One can see oneself going through mental fluctuations that arise from a constant interaction between the mind, intellect, ego, and the world outside. In the very beginning of his *Yoga Sutra,* Patanjali states: "To control these mental fluctuations is Yoga." Control of these mental modifications is only possible by controlling *prana.* Therefore, the control of *prana,* called *pranayama,* is the primary step in the spiritual path of Yoga. Yoga offers instruction in spiritual practices *(sadhana)* which make an aspirant the best friend of his or her own body.

This book is about the practices of Tantra Yoga, also called Maha Yoga, the primary origin of the system of working with chakras and the dormant Kundalini energy. Through yogic practice, one gains the ability to expend the least possible physiochemical energy for mentation and to maintain the body's vitality. That enables one to divert pranic (of *prana*) energy to activate one's dormant spiritual energy, called Kundalini. This energy in its dormant state is visualized as a snake coiled up in the first chakra at the base of the spine, the Muladhara Chakra.

When an aspirant *(sadhaka)* of Yoga starts activating the Kundalini energy through various kinds of *pranayamas,* the Nadi system is vitalized. The roused energy moves upward in the central Nadi, the Sushumna, passing through each of the six lower chakras to reach the seventh, the Sahasrara Chakra. This progress is known as *kshata chakra bhedana* (piercing of the six chakras). The release and ascent of the dormant spiritual energy enables the aspirant to transcend the effects of the elements and achieve the nondual consciousness that brings liberation from the ever-changing world of illusion *(maya).*

Some teachers and spiritual guides, healers, and Western thinkers say that playing with "chakra-stuff" is dangerous and that the sudden arousal of Kundalini without proper preparation can create problems. They scare people unnecessarily. As we shall see in chapter 2, "Kundalini and Yoga," the rousing of Kundalini is the activation of upward-moving energy. It is true that the ascent of Kundalini is associated with the withdrawal of *prana* and the suspension of breathing, which can be achieved with the practice of *pranayama.* However, unless one employs other yogic practices, that suspension of breath is temporary, ending with the next inhalation. Those who wish to work with meditation on the chakras should not worry; the Kundalini energy is not aroused by meditation alone. Even if it is aroused, its ascent will not endanger the living organism. It should also be noted that the sudden arousal of Kundalini by extreme emotions such as intense joy or sorrow can happen to anyone at any time. The energies in the body are always working, but if one can work with them at will, as we shall learn in this book, one will have more freedom.

The teachings in this book come from my father, who practiced the piercing of the six chakras *(kshata chakra bhedana),* and from different tantric scriptures, the writings of saints, and various scrolls that depict the chakras in a number of different ways. To assist in understanding the ancient concepts I have added many drawings and charts with the hope of enriching people's knowledge and helping them to comprehend the age-old Indian tradition of Tantra in a modern context.

Each of the figures drawn in this book are facsimiles of illustrated Tantric texts and scrolls. The chakra figures are a language in and of themselves and aid the aspirant in visualizing the chakras. A description accompanies each chakra explaining the symbolism drawn in the figures. Concentration on physical organs or locations, as prescribed by many spiritual masters, is misleading, for the chakras are not material. Thus the figures given here are an invaluable device for one trying to visualize chakras while meditating on them.

One of the twin hemispheres in the human brain is visual and the other verbal. The visual hemisphere works with the images of the chakras presented in the illustrations, which have been especially designed for coloring. The true aspirant is best advised to concentrate on the deities of the chakras which represent different aspects of consciousness, and thus come into contact with those states of consciousness that are characteristic for each chakra. The verbal hemisphere is engaged when the seed sounds *(bija mantras)* that are connected with each of the chakras are simultaneously repeated. Through repetition of the seed sounds, the deities which are present in sound form become alive and the aspirant can experience their presence.

Using the faculties of hearing and sight together *(mantra* and *yantra)* is *tantra.* One subtly receives information and inspiration from the forms, colors, and sounds. One can make the body a true asset by training one's sensory and motor organs with the discipline given by yogic practices involving the breath, the repetition of special sounds *(mantra japa),* and concentration. One who masters this practice will find himself or herself in a meditative state while being neither inert nor inactive.

Tantra has studied chakras as centers of transformation in all walks of life and has evolved the system of Tantra Yoga to bring happiness and joy in worldly life as well as spiritual evolution. Tantra Yoga is for anybody who has a spine, two nostrils, good concentration, and the power of visualization.

Principles of Tantra Yoga

The scriptures of Tantra Yoga are dialogues between Shiva, the infinite supreme consciousness, and Shakti, the divine mother, the eternal energy of the supreme consciousness. When Shakti becomes manifest as Shiva's counterpart to enact his divine *lila* (sport, play) in time and space, she asks him questions about methods to live in peace and how to use one's lifetime in a fruitful manner. Knowing that people with only common insight have difficulty in grasping the truth of the sacred *(vedic)* teachings, Shiva simplifies and modifies them. By incorporating new processes and practices, he makes the teachings more adaptable, practical, absorbing, powerful, and accessible to a larger number of the divine mother's beloved children. This simplified version of the sacred teachings was termed Tantra Yoga by the followers of Shakti.

In Tantra Yoga the aspirant has to see himself or herself as a microcosm. Then it is not necessary to search for anything outside of oneself; the body is one's instrument. The journey is not outside but inside, starting from the Muladhara Chakra, one's own base, where spiritual energy is dormant and coiled up. This spiritual energy is the divine mother Shakti herself in the form of Kundalini. She is longing for union with her beloved, the supreme Shiva, who is in eternal bliss in the Sahasrara Chakra at the top of the cranium. Her arousal is delayed by the constant mental activity that draws the aspirant to the world of sense perception in search of the satisfaction of his or her desires. In everyday life, the mind is usually involved with material existence and does not go beyond the sensory boundary. It perceives the world, thinks, wills, desires, and feels pleasures and pains. It serves the I-consciousness. Tantric practices lead the mind to its higher aspect where it completely closes its doors to the world and does not desire, think, or will, but it realizes the supreme truth and thus merges into the supreme consciousness.

Tantra is a practical approach to the truth that is beyond words. It deals with a person's psychophysical energy: first directing it to function correctly and then transforming that energy into spiritual energy, so that a direct experience of truth becomes possible. Tantra knows that the human organism is capable of realizing truth beyond the realm of sensory perception. With the help of memory, imagination, and intuition, a person can grasp the laws of nature and can put otherwise mysterious forces to work for one's benefit, growth, and development. With the perfect synchronization of interior and exterior rhythms, one can follow the path of least resistance and float freely in the ocean of the phenomenal world without getting drowned. To be precise, the human body is the most perfect instrument for the expression of consciousness.

The chief centers of consciousness in human beings are found in the cerebrospinal system and in the upper brain. The cerebrospinal system is the first part of the organism to be developed after conception. From it the entire bodily form materializes. This system is a great generator of electrical energy and has a fantastic network of nerves that serve as connectors. The cerebrum, as the upper brain is called, continuously produces electrical energy. Through nerves this energy is constantly supplied to the organism, providing life force. At the back and at the base of the skull is the cerebellum—the lower brain, the organ of the subconscious mind. This is also known as the mechanical brain, the cobra brain, or the reptile brain. The upper brain, a comparatively later development than the lower brain, is more open to change.

The functioning of the entire human body is controlled by the cerebrospinal system, and the chakras are activated through this system. For many centuries knowledge of these psychic centers has been handed down through the Hindu tantric tradition. The yogic belief is that for balanced functioning, proper harmony should exist between the two brains: the upper brain (the organism of consciousness) and the lower brain (the seat of the subconscious mind).

Andha Kupa
The tenth gate
Seat of supreme
consciousness

Cerebral cortex (upper brain)
Inspiration and free thinking
associated with the sixth and
seventh chakras (and minor
chakras within the seventh)

Midbrain
Emotions and finer sentiments
associated with the fourth, fifth,
and sixth chakras

Brain stem (lower brain)
Genetic code and basic instincts
associated with the five lower
chakras

Diagram of the brain, its functions, and its relationship to the chakras

Modern studies of the upper and lower brains point toward inner conflict
between the two and relate this conflict to behavioral patterns that are influenced and affected by it. These studies also point toward a basic dichotomy
in human nature. This dichotomy is further substantiated by the presence of
twin hemispheres in the upper brain (the cerebrum). Human beings dwell in
this duality and become victims of endless problems and complexes. To resolve
this dichotomy, the most practical and plausible solution seems to be to create a
union between the upper and lower brain, and between the brain's right and left
hemispheres. Balanced union is achieved through constant work on all four of
these components. Thus a basic requirement for spiritual development is a sys-

tematic study of the activities and functions of the human organism at work.

Many scientific investigations have been based on the study of dead or sick bodies from which living or healthy data is not obtained. In contrast, the ancient sciences of Tantra and Yoga have made holistic studies of the healthy human organism. The results of their research, however, have not yet been broadly correlated with the experimentations and explorations of Western medicine. Recently, though, there has been a greater acceptance and broader application of exercise and breath control in post-operative and preventive measures, practices that have been translated directly from the tantric and yogic traditions and successfully adapted for the benefit of modern people. However, in order to attain a full understanding of the human being, the psychic dimensions—not simply the physical ones—must be examined thoroughly.

It is believed that the system through which transcendental union was first successfully sought is Yoga. The word *yoga* is derived from the Sanskrit root *yuj,* which means "to unite," "to join," "to add." If considered at the gross physical level, the union is between the upper brain and the lower brain, the conscious with the subconscious. At a subtle level the union is between one's individual consciousness and cosmic consciousness (that is, the soul uniting with God). Yoga presents a system that creates the state of unification of mental processes and consciousness. Yoga is based on particular disciplines and exercises through which union of individual and cosmic consciousness may be obtained by anyone who chooses to adhere to the prescribed system. According to Yoga, individual consciousness is an expression of cosmic consciousness, divine reality, the source, the substratum of the manifested universe. In essence, cosmic consciousness and individual consciousness are one, because both are consciousness, which is indivisible. But the two are separated by subjectivity, the I-consciousness of the individual. Realization of one's divine nature brings release from the trap of one's animal nature, which causes subjectivity and limited vision. In the language of Yoga this is called the "mind trap." Only after the dissolution of the individual consciousness does union with cosmic consciousness take place.

The term "mind" is used in an entirely different context in Yoga than it is in modern psychology where it denotes the functional aspect of the brain that is responsible for thought, volition, and feelings. The brain is considered to be a material reality that is a tool of the mind, but the mind itself is not materially real. Thus modern scientists engage in the search for a non-material reality in the material brain and its twin hemispheres. They search for the psyche. The core of ancient wisdom sheds much light on this subject and, if aptly researched and correlated, has much to offer in this field. In the realms of modern psychology and modern medical science the ancient insights have been understood to a certain extent. And to a degree, some scientists are doing pioneering research on the correlations between this ancient knowledge and their own observations.

In this day and age we are seeking harmony between the rational approach and the emotional or devotional approach to the human psyche. The methods employed by the two systems—the modern and the ancient—have a basic difference in their approach. Yogis approach the psyche by searching for its cause in the mind and consciousness. Psychologists, on the other hand, seek to define it by studying behavior. The original yogic formula is to discover the Self through self-research; the approach of scientists today is to observe others and not the Self, which is in everybody. Psychologists and other scientists involved with understanding consciousness study individuals and groups to determine the various dimensions of the mind. Yoga not only describes all mental states, aspects, and dimensions possible within the individual, but also advocates practical games to be played with the mind to control its functioning, to achieve peace, and to free a person from the miseries and suffering caused by mental fluctuations and modifications. Inherent in Yoga are practical devices through which one may go beyond the mind's normal way of functioning.

Apart from its significance in the spiritual development of the individual, the philosophy of Yoga has a moral value and is very useful in daily life. In yogic principles lies the foundation for better human relationships and collective peace. A basic yogic concept is stated in the maxim: "May all be happy, may all be in peace" *(Sarve bhavantu sukhina, sarve sant niramaya)*.

Principles established by yogic philosophy are universal and provide scope for the overall development and advancement of all faculties of the mind. They provide the aspirant who works through Yoga the ability to stop all mental modifications at will. The constant practice of self-restraint helps the aspirant to become centered and quiet. It also quiets the inner dialogue without effort. The fruit of yogic practice *(sadhana)* is the ability to rise above afflictions and to transcend the cognitive faculties, the perceptual world, and the attachment to the body and the senses. It provides the mind with habitual one-pointedness, undivided attention, perpetual peace, change in behavioral patterns, and, finally, enlightenment.

One-pointedness is an attribute especially useful in this fast-paced, high-tech age. Peace within and around us, without distractions or disturbances, is essential to self-expression. Individually we need to understand our latent potential. We need self-discovery. We further need to understand ourselves as a microcosm, and to understand our relationship with the macrocosm. All physical sciences tend to divide reality into many parts, whereas spiritual sciences focus on and perceive unity in diversity. Although it is indeed necessary to study part by part, it is also necessary to create a whole from those parts and to recognize one's own place in relation to that of others, who are similar parts. Too much individualism, subjectivity, and attention to one's own interests creates veils and closes the windows of open-mindedness. An overemphasis on the individual self fosters feelings of loneliness and pessimism. Acknowledging this, the system of Yoga has identified five states of mind classification.

The Five States of Mind

1. Autism *(kshipta)*
In this state one has neither the patience nor the intelligence necessary for contemplation of a super-sensuous object and consequently cannot think of nor comprehend any subtle principle. Through intense envy or malice, the mind may at times be in a state of concentration, but this is not yogic concentration.

2. Stupefaction *(mudha)*
In this state of mind, obsession with a matter connected with the senses renders one unfit to think of subtle principles. An example is someone engrossed in thoughts of family or wealth to the point of infatuation.

3. Restlessness *(vyagra)*
This state is not to be equated with the *kshipta* state. Most spiritual devotees basically have this type of mind—a mind that may be calm sometimes and

disturbed at other times. When temporarily calm, a restless mind may understand the real nature of subtle principles when it hears of them and can contemplate on them for an extended period. Although concentration is possible with a restless mind, it is not long-lasting. Liberation cannot be secured through concentration alone when the mind is habitually restless, because when concentration ceases, distraction arises again. Until the mind is free of distractions and a permanent one-pointedness develops, the state of salvation is impossible to achieve.

4. One-pointedness *(ekagra)*

Patanjali, the compiler of the *Yoga Sutras,* has defined this as a state of mind wherein, on the fading away of one thought, another thought follows in succession with the previous thought; when there is a continuous succession of such thoughts, the mind is called "one-pointed." Slowly it becomes a habit of the mind in waking consciousness, and even in the dream state. When one-pointedness is mastered, one attains super-conscious concentration *(samprajnata samadhi).* This *samadhi* (realized nonduality) is true yogic *samadhi,* leading to salvation.

5. Suppression *(niruddha)*

This is the state devoid of thought. By constant practice of the cessation of thoughts, one can truly understand the world of names and forms as a product of the mind. When the mind ceases to exist in a practical sense of the term, all else dissolves. This is the unconscious-conscious state of blissful illumination *(asamaprajnata samadhi).*

These states of mind make the person we experience. The person is the mind, and the mind is the person. Thus the study of the mind is the study of the person and vice versa. Yoga uses mental processes and psychological efforts to get the aspirant out of the "mind-trap." It stops the mental modifications and fluctuations which are the progenitors of the different states of mind. That is why it is said that Yoga is not a physical activity of the body, it is a mental process.

Lord Shiva expounded twelve forms of Yoga:

1. Mantra Yoga	5. Bhakti Yoga	9. Vasana Yoga
2. Hatha Yoga	6. Kriya Yoga	10. Para Yoga
3. Laya Yoga	7. Gyana Yoga	11. Amanaska Yoga
4. Raja Yoga	8. Lakshya Yoga	12. Sahaj Yoga

The Four Yogas of Tantra Yoga

Tantra Yoga, also called Maha (the great) Yoga, is a combination of the four main Yogas:

1. Mantra Yoga

The word *mantra* is a combination of two words. *Man* means "mind" *(manas)*. *Man* also comes from *manan* which means "concentration." *Tra* comes from *trana* which means "freedom" and "protection." Thus *mantra* is that which enables our consciousness to become free from worldly thoughts and to go into a state of concentration. By the power of sound inherent in a mantra the mind becomes controlled and concentration becomes well established.

Sound precedes all existence. The element *akasha* is produced by sound; then the rest of the elements *(bhutas* or *tattvas)*—air, fire, water, and earth—are produced by *akasha*. Sound in its essence is divine and represents cosmic consciousness in whichever form the aspirant desires divinity to take. This divine form is intrinsically related to the seed sound *(bija mantra)*. The *Yoga Shikhopanishad* (verses 2 to 9) states that Kundalini manifests herself as mantra. By the yogic process of mantra repetition *(mantra japa)* the sounds are converted into the divine form of Kundalini power and revealed to the aspirant.

Mantra Yoga is not only the repetition of a mantra or seed sound *(bija mantra)*. The correct intonation of a mantra enables concentration to gradually become deep and uninterrupted. At a higher stage of deep concentration, the divine form *(devata)* inherent in the mantra becomes manifest. When the *devata* becomes living, the I-consciousness merges into the divinity of the mantra and the aspirant reaches the state of *samadhi*.

2. Hatha Yoga

The word *hatha* is a combination of two sounds, *ha* and *tha*. *Ha* stands for the sun and *tha* for the moon. *Hatha* thus is balance and the union of the sun and moon. Through practice of different postures *(asanas)* and breath control *(pranayama)* this Yoga energizes the subtle channels, the Yoga Nadis. Energy moves through these channels without any obstruction because each and every cell of the body has been cleansed by the purificatory practices of Hatha Yoga. A body thus trained does not present any obstacles to the state of concentration or meditation which leads to *samadhi*.

3. Laya Yoga

Laya means "dissolution" or "absorption." According to the *Rudrayamala Tantra*, Laya Yoga is also called Kundalini Yoga and *kshata chakra yoga*. When Kundalini, the supreme power *(adi shakti),* remains coiled in an individual organism, mundaneness arises in consciousness. Every individual is under the influence of the cosmic creative principles: the five elements; the five essential principles *(tanmatras);* the five senses and their objects; the five organs of action; the will; and the inner organ *(antahkarana)* made up of the mind *(manas),* the intellect *(buddhi),* the I-consciousness *(ahamkara),* and the feeling self *(chitta).* Laya Yoga believes that the realization of supreme consciousness is not possible until all the cosmic creative principles are absorbed into the spiritual aspect of the supreme consciousness, Param Shiva. Thus the methods of arousing Kundalini and uniting her with Param Shiva are the essential part of Laya Yoga. The cosmic creative principles are absorbed stage by stage into Kundalini through deep meditation *(dhyana).* This energized spiritual consciousness is then absorbed in the supreme consciousness, resulting in *samadhi.*

4. Raja Yoga

Raja means "royal," so Raja Yoga is also called the royal path of Yoga. Raja Yoga believes that by suspension of the thinking principle, one is able to achieve union at will. It aims at purifying the consciousness to the highest degree and transforming it into the state of super-conscious concentration *(samprajnata samadhi).* By stopping the mental modifications *(vritti nirodha),* one reaches the state of *samprajnata samadhi* without any effort. The final goal of Raja Yoga is for this super-purified and super-illuminated consciousness to become completely absorbed into supreme consciousness *(asamprajnata samadhi).*

Raja Yoga does not awaken the dormant power of Kundalini. In Raja Yoga, centralized thought combined with spiritual reflection is applied for the attainment of the withdrawal from sensory perceptions *(pratyahara),* which causes *prana* to withdraw sensory control. The sense organs are withdrawn as they are withdrawn during sleep. This leads to deep meditation *(dhyana)* and *samadhi.*

All four of these Yogas are a part of Tantra Yoga, and each in their own way approaches the same goal. When all four are combined and the aspirant selects from each system what he or she needs, the aspirant is practicing Maha Yoga (the great Yoga). Maha Yoga places utmost importance on working with *prana,* the vital life force through which all that is manifest survives. In Ayurveda, the Indian science of medicine, the word *prana* is used to indicate the humor called *vata dosha* or *vayu* (air). *Prana* carries the vital force, needed for keeping the system alive, as well as chemical wastes and toxins which need to be expelled out of the body. Through various kinds of breathing techniques, *prana* is used to cleanse the nerves and to arouse the dormant energy (Kundalini). In nature *prana* is one, but Yoga divides it into five sub-classes according to its location and type of movement in the human body.

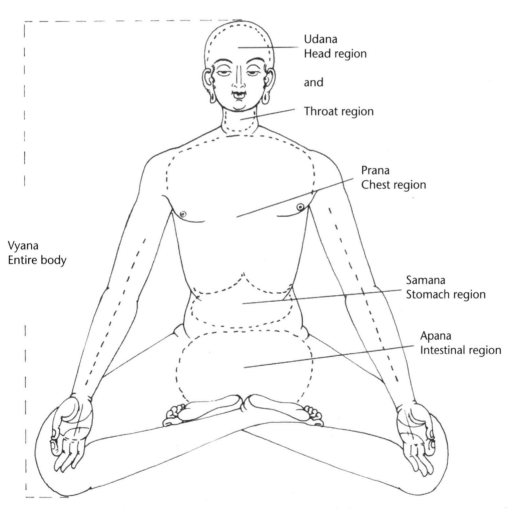

Udana
Head region

and

Throat region

Prana
Chest region

Vyana
Entire body

Samana
Stomach region

Apana
Intestinal region

Pranas *in the body*

The Five *Pranas* or *Vayus*

1. *Udana*

Udana dwells in the throat and head region. It is with the power of *udana* that one gains the ability to produce sound in the form of speech, music, and humming. It helps the aspirant in *mantra japa* (repetition).

2. *Prana*

Prana operates in the heart and lungs, and in the air that is constantly moving in and out of the nasal passages. It helps in swallowing and brings food and drink into the stomach. It is the primary life breath. By slowing down the rate of breathing to fifteen breaths per minute, it is possible to change the speed of the mind; by rhythmic breathing with *mantra japa,* the aspirant of Yoga can achieve a state of tranquillity.

3. *Samana*

Samana resides in the region between the heart and naval. It maintains the stomach "fire" with the help of the digestive juices. *Samana* cooks the food and separates nutrients from waste matter.

4. *Apana*

Apana dwells in the area between the navel and rectum. The primary function of *apana* is to discharge the waste materials produced in the process of digestion and assimilation of food. It is also responsible for flatulence, ejaculation, conception, delivery, defecation, and urination. Its role in the movement of Kundalini, the opening of Brahma Nadi, and spiritual experiences makes it more important than *udana* and *vyana*.

5. *Vyana*

Vyana dwells in the whole body and circulates continuously throughout the body through the blood vessels, the lymphatic system, and the nervous system. Because it regulates the three basic systems (circulatory, lymphatic, and nervous), it is the most universal and significant. It carries nutrients, makes blood flow, causes sweating, cleans toxins from the blood and lymph, and helps in the coordination of all the systems. Getting up, sitting down, pushing, pulling, opening and closing the eyes, is all done by *vyana*. It helps in *asanas* and the withdrawal of the senses.

Tantra Yoga believes *prana* to be the key to all spiritual experiences. It is said in *Shiva Svarodaya*:

Nadibhedam tatha pranatattva bhedam tathaiv cha
Sushumna mishra bhedam cha yo janati sa-muktigah

One who knows the secrets of the Nadis (their operation and effect), of *prana*, and of Sushumna gets liberated from the cycle of life and death, being totally enlightened.

Tantra Yoga works with the dynamic *prana* energy which the organism receives through nasal breathing. According to tantric teachings, two of the major Yoga Nadis (carriers of subtle energy in the body) terminate in the nostrils. The Ida Nadi terminates in the left nostril and is activated by breath in that nostril. The Pingala Nadi terminates and is activated by breath in the right nostril. When both nostrils work simultaneously, the major Yoga Nadi called the Sushumna becomes active, creating coordination between the right and left sides of the body.

Typically a human being breathes at an average rate of fifteen breaths per minute or 900 times an hour. Out of that, 890 breaths are taken with one nostril or the other, activating either the Ida Nadi or the Pingala Nadi. Only ten breaths per hour are taken with both nostrils working together, thus activating the Sushumna Nadi. However, the use of alternative breathing techniques taught by Yoga enables an aspirant to activate the Sushumna at will. The subtle energy centers of the chakras are situated in the Sushumna Nadi, working with the dynamic *prana* energy which is in constant motion in the Nadi-field.

The Sushumna Nadi has a very delicate Nadi inside of it called Brahma Nadi, which is the carrier of spiritual energy. The joint operation of the right and left nostrils that occurs naturally each hour stimulates the Sushumna Nadi but it does not stimulate the Brahma Nadi. The Brahma Nadi is influenced only when the Sushumna is activated by *pranayama* (conscious breath control). Then the spiritual energy which is dormant in the sleeping Kundalini is aroused to move upward through the Brahma Nadi. When the dormant spiritual energy is roused, the working of the physiochemical energy stops and the body becomes calm and motionless. Dynamic *prana* is absorbed in the aroused Kundalini energy. One's metabolism decreases and vital functions of the body stop. In the end the sensory system stops functioning. Kundalini moves through the hollow path inside the vertebral column, passing through the chakras, the centers of transformation. Piercing all of the lower chakras, she ultimately reaches the Sahasrara Chakra where she unites with her beloved Shiva.

After this union Kundalini goes back to her abode in the Muladhara Chakra at the base of the spine. During her descent, the powers and operations of the chakras are restored. The aspirant or yogi returns to working, time-bound, I-consciousness, and the cyclical operation of the three well-known states of consciousness—the waking state, the dream state, and the sleep state of consciousness—which are influenced by the three *gunas* (qualities): *sattva* (equanimity, balance, or lightness), *rajas* (passion, activity, or mobility), and *tamas* (sloth, inertia, or darkness).

The Different States of Consciousness

1. The Waking State

In the waking state of consciousness, the mind, the intellect, the ego, and the feeling self are constantly active, making consciousness in this state appear to be sense consciousness. When I-consciousness operates under the influence of *rajas,* the sensory impulses of smell, taste, sight, touch, and sound are received by the sensory area of the brain. These sensory impulses are reduced to a non-material form as *vayu* (air) or *prana*. They are then transported through the Ida Nadi to their corresponding chakra. Each of the first five chakras is associated with one of the five senses and sensory organs and the element that organ is connected with. For example, the Muladhara Chakra is associated with the sense of smell, the nose, and the earth element. The sensory impulses in the form of *prana* are radiated through the petals of their particular chakra to the Ida Nadi and thence to the sense mind. The sense mind sends the sensory-mental radiations to the I-consciousness (ego) and the *chitta* (feeling self), where they are changed into conscious forms that the I-consciousness recognizes as smells, tastes, sights, touches, and sounds.

2. The Dream State

The dream world is created by impressions, memories, and desires (fulfilled or unfulfilled), projected on the screen of the I-consciousness. The dream state appears to be a state of non-consciousness because the sensory area of the brain is inoperative. If seen by others, the person will be described as sleeping, but the dream state is dominated by *rajas* and *sattva,* not *tamas. Rajas* makes the sense mind function even without the help of the sense organs, and the light of *sattva* makes things without any material form seem to appear. One smells without using the nose, tastes without using the tongue, sees without using the eyes, feels and hears without the activity of the skin and the ears. Although the sense organs are inoperative there is complete involvement of the I-consciousness with the dream world.

3. The Sleep State

When the sense organs and the sense mind become inoperative, sense consciousness becomes masked, giving rise to apparent non-consciousness. This happens when the I-consciousness operates under the influence of *tamas. Tamas* brings on dullness, drowsiness, ignorance, lack of meaning, and stupidity. The sense organs withdraw from the external realm to become perfectly introverted. Sleep helps to restore energy to the body, which it consumes in the following day's cycle of activity. In the sleep state, the mind, the ego, and the intellect are absorbed in the feeling self *(chitta),* and the *chitta* is merged in the supreme consciousness *(Param Shiva)* within the human organism.

4. Turiya

Besides these three states, there is a fourth state of consciousness known as *turiya.* This is the state in which the supreme spirit is seen through super-consciousness. Through concentration, the mind, ego, intellect, and sense consciousness are all absorbed and a state of undifferentiated consciousness prevails. When the *gunas (sattva, rajas,* and *tamas)* are absorbed in the spiritual energy, Kundalini, there is neither consciousness nor unconsciousness. That is the state of *samprajnata samadhi.* This state has been recently recognized by modern psychology as the "altered state of consciousness." Then comes the highest state known as *asamprajnata samadhi* where Kundalini herself is absorbed into the Supreme Shiva, the cosmic consciousness.

One who has experienced *turiya* sees the same world differently thereafter. Percepts are the same but one's perspective changes. Fear, pain, suffering, and bondage lose their meaning because all types of bondage are caused by attachment stemming from desire. *Turiya* creates detachment; all desires disappear and one experiences the freedom that a drop experiences after it merges into the ocean. But this happens only when the coiled spiritual energy of Kundalini is aroused by following the practices given in detail in the following chapters.

Kundalini and Yoga

The word *kundalini* comes from the Sanskrit word *kundal,* which means a "spiral" or "coil." In Yoga, *Kundalini Shakti* means the "coiled power." It is compared to a serpent that lies coiled while resting or sleeping.

There are numerous references to Kundalini in the sacred texts of India. Shankaracharya, in his famous treatise, *Saundarya Lahari,* says: "The invincible Kundalini Shakti pierces the six chakras and enters its abode slowly step by step." In the *Mundamalatantra* (ch. 6), Kundalini Shakti is called the basic force of the body. In the *Varahopanishad* (5.51), Kundalini is called the supreme power. In the *Yogashikhopanishad* (6.55) it is stated that when Kundalini Shakti rises above its resting point (the *kanda*), the yogi attains liberation. In the *Yajurveda,* Kundalini is mentioned as a virgin energy which moves like a devoted wife and destroys all evils, and, by its slight movement, through its fiery energy, pierces all centers. Also in the *Yajurveda* it is said:

Kundalini shakteravasth trayam vidyate
Yaddyasmin chakre kumari kumaravathamapanta
Prathmam supto itthta mandryete mandam swaram karoti
Purum hiranyamayim brahma vivesho parajita

Three states of Kundalini Shakti can be seen. In her initial virgin state she stays youthful in her resting place. First she is in her dormant sleeping form, then slow movement and mild sound starts. Then she, fully illuminated, enters the cave of Brahma, where she unites and loses herself.

In the *Yogakundalyupanishad* it is said:

Kundale asyah stah iti kundalini
Muladharasth vanhiyatm tejo madhye vyavasthita
Jivashakti kundalakhya pranakarath tejasa
Mahakundalini prokta parabrahma swarupini
Shabda brahma maye devi ekoanekakshara kriti
Shakti kundalininam vistantunibha shubha

One which is a coiled form [*kundal*] is the Kundalini. In the Muladhara she stays in the form of fire, which is surrounded by luminosity. She is the *Jiva Shakti* [individualized consciousness] and is known as Kundalini. She is full of luminosity [*tejas*] and is the cause of *prana,* the vital life force. When she is in the Supreme Being, the Para Brahma, she is called Maha Kundalini. Devi Kundalini is of the form of Shabda Brahma [*shabda* - sound, *brahma* - god without name and form]. Goddess Kundalini herself is the Supreme Being as sound and has a form of one and many alphabet characters [she exists in mantra form]. The auspicious Kundalini Shakti exists in every particle in her own way.

There are many other references to Kundalini in *Gyanarva Tantra, Lalita Sahastranam, Laghustuti Vamkeshwar Tantra, Kshata Chakra Nirupana, Gheranya Samhita,* and *Hatha Yogpradipika* in which she is described as an aspect of the eternal supreme consciousness, which is both with and without attributes. In the aspect of supreme consciousness with attributes *(saguna),* Kundalini is often personified as an aspect of the Divine Mother, the Great Goddess. In the attributeless aspect *(nirguna),* Kundalini is the power or will of cosmic consciousness and is pure consciousness.

In the tantric tradition the universe is believed to be made up basically of two things: the *saguna* (with attributes) and the *nirguna* (without attributes) or, in another manner of speaking, matter and energy. Matter is treated as the vehicle of energy, and energy is considered to be consciousness (not like the energy of modern scientists, which is devoid of consciousness). Before manifestation there is only supreme consciousness without attributes (Shiva) and the power of consciousness (Kundalini or Shakti). When Shiva and Shakti come together, there is the thrill of union *(nada),* and from this the *maha bindu* is born. *Nada* is pure cosmic sound and *maha bindu* is the supreme truth that is the seed of all manifest phenomena. According to the tantric scripture *Sharada Tilak,* manifestation begins with the bursting of the *bindu.* First there was unmanifest sound *(shabda* or *nada),* the Word. ("In the beginning there was the Word, and the Word was God.") Inherent in the Word is the energy *(shakti)* of its meanings *(artha).* Through the action of volition *(kriya),* the unmanifest sound becomes the source of the manifest word.

The bursting of the *bindu* is the beginning of differentiation. From the differentiating *bindu,* the material universe evolves in the form of the *tattvas,* the eternal verities. An eternal verity may be defined as "that energy which gives scope for functioning to all orders of creation, till their final dissolution." Tantra classifies the eternal verities in three groups: *Atma* (self) *Tattvas, Vidya* (knowledge) *Tattvas,* and *Shiva* (consciousness) *Tattvas.* The eternal energies that comprise the first group, the *Atma Tattvas,* are characterized by non-sentience *(jada).* The eternal verities of the second group, the *Vidya Tattvas,* combine non-sentience *(jada)* with illumination *(prakasha),* resulting in sentience, pure and simple. The *Shiva Tattvas* are characterized by illumination *(prakasha)* with absolute consciousness standing above them all. There are seven categories of existence within the *Vidya Tattva,* including Kundalini, and five categories within the *Shiva Tattva,* including *prana,* the creator of all.

According to the tantric scripture *Kalpa Sutra,* twenty-four categories of non-sentient existence are within the first group of eternal verities, the *Atma Tattvas.* These may be arranged as shown below with their characteristic qualities:

1. *Prithvi* – earth, possessed of solidity

2. *Apah* – water, possessed of fluidity

3. *Tejas* – fire, possessed of heat

4. *Vayu* – air, possessed of the quality of perpetual motion

5. *Akasha* – void, possessed of the character of space

6. *Gandha tanmatra* – smell, in the form of subtle earth

7. *Rasa tanmatra* – taste, in the form of subtle water

8. *Rupa tanmatra* – form, in the form of subtle fire

9. *Sparsha tanmatra* – touch, in the form of subtle air

10. *Shabda tanmatra* – sound, in the form of subtle *akasha*

11. *Srota* – ear, the auditory sense of perceiving sound

12. *Tvac* – skin, the tactile sense that perceives touch

13. *Chakshu* – eye, the optic sense that perceives form

14. *Jihva* – tongue, the gustatory sense that perceives taste

15. *Ghrana* – nose, the olfactory sense that perceives smell

16. *Vac* – speech, tongue, the motor organ of articulate expression

17. *Pani* – the hand, the motor organ of grasping and leaving

18. *Pada* – the foot, the motor organ of locomotion

19. *Payu* – anus, the motor organ of evacuation

20. *Upastha* – the genital, the motor organ of generation and casual pleasure

21. *Manas* – the mind, the inner sense that is the root of all volition, which is attained when the misery of mobility *(rajas)* prevails over the balanced rhythm of happiness *(sattva)* and the inertia of delusion *(tamas)*

22. *Buddhi* – the intellect, the inner sense that is the root of all conviction, which is attained when balance and clarity *(sattva)* prevail over mobility *(rajas)* and inertia *(tamas)*

23. *Ahamkara* – egoism, the I-consciousness, the inner sense that is the root of all fancy converging toward the Self, which is attained when inertia or darkness *(tamas)* prevails over balance *(sattva)* and mobility *(rajas)*

24. *Prakriti* – primordial nature, being, otherwise known as *chitta,* which is attained by the equipoised state of the three qualities *(gunas): sattva, rajas,* and *tamas.*

The culmination of the evolution of creation is in the individuated self (called *jiva, purusha,* or *atma*), which gives the scope of functioning to the twenty-four non-sentient categories. It does so by using the four internal work organs of consciousness known as *antah karana chatushtaya:* the mind *(manas),* the intellect *(buddhi),* the ego or I-consciousness *(ahamkara),* and the feeling self, being, or nature *(chitta).* With the combined help of these four organs, the gross material body, which is composed of uncountable cells, becomes a single unit of existence, "one body."

The *jiva* is kept in contact with the entire order of creation through *prana,* the vital life force which comes as breath. All kinds of knowledge *(vidya)* in the form of different energies exist in the body. Thus, Kundalini *sadhana* (discipline), particularly the control of *prana (pranayama),* is the primary tantric *sadhana* through which all *vidyas* become known to the *jiva.* In a reversal of the evolution of the manifested phenomenal world, all of the cosmic creative principles are reabsorbed in Kundalini one by one. Ultimately, Kundalini is the means by which the individual consciousness is absorbed into the Param Shiva (supreme consciousness) of the *Shiva Tattva,* and nondual consciousness is attained.

Until that union with supreme consciousness, all creatures act through the power of Kundalini Shakti. The ceaseless movement of the forces of the body is Shakti in her kinetic aspect. Kundalini at rest at the base of the spine in the Muladhara Chakra is the immobile support of all these operations. In individual organisms, the energized consciousness or conscious energy exists in five sheaths *(koshas)* and operates through the physical body.

The Five Sheaths *(Koshas)*

1. *Annamayi Kosha* – Sheath of Matter

The *Annamayi Kosha* is the cellular body. With the help of *prana, Annamayi Kosha* creates the foundation of the body. All of the material contents of *Atma Tattva* are created by *prana,* but the stuff from which the material contents evolve is *anna,* food.

2. *Pranamayi Kosha* – Sheath of Vital Air *(Prana)*

The next sheath is the *Pranamayi Kosha,* the support of all mental, super-mental, and psychic energy, and individual consciousness. *Prana* maintains the life force in the cellular body through food which is converted into different kinds of energy through the three humors *(doshas): vayu, pitta, kapha. Vayu* is air or wind from the air element, which works in the body as the five *pranas (prana, apana, samana, vyana,* and *udana)* and as five sub-*pranas (kurma, krikil, naga, dhananjaye,* and *devdutta),* and directly influences all movements in the body.

3. *Manomayi Kosha* – Sheath of Mind

Prana also maintains vitality in the *Manomayi Kosha,* the mental body, through the chemical soup prepared by *Annamayi Kosha,* which creates different moods *(rasas)* in the I-consciousness. Tantra describes nine different moods or *rasas* that are played out in the psychodrama of life. The variety of feelings and emotions generated by the interaction of the *rasas* with the I-consciousness gives a definite character to the *jiva* of the microcosm.

4. *Vijnanamayi Kosha* – Sheath of Knowledge

Next to *Manomayi Kosha* is *Vijnanamayi Kosha.* This is the sheath of knowledge beyond sensory perception. This sheath is the seat of *buddhi* (intellect) and *ahamkara* (I-consciousness). The mind presents the messages from the phenomenal world to the intellect, the adviser that has a record of all that has happened in the past and all the possibilities of the future. It is conscious of the positive and negative aspects of everything the mind presents, and always perceives through a three-dimensional framework of the past, present, and future. In individual consciousness, the intellect and ego are time-bound. Only the Self—the pure consciousness in individual consciousness—is beyond time, ego, and intellect. This Self is the Param Shiva, which always stays in the middle of the game board of life in its own sheath, *Anandamayi Kosha,* the Sheath of Bliss.

5. *Anandamayi Kosha* – Sheath of Bliss

The Self, undaunted by pleasure and pain, stays in bliss in this sheath. This Self is the nondual cosmic consciousness—omnipresent, omnipotent, and omniscient. Being omnipresent, it has to be everywhere, yet it is in the sheath of *ananda* which is surrounded by all the other sheaths of its own divine *maya* (the veiling power; the ever-changing illusory existence, the phenomenon).

The mind and even *prana* cannot reach the energized consciousness of *Anandamayi Kosha.* Only *chitta,* the pure being of individualized consciousness, is

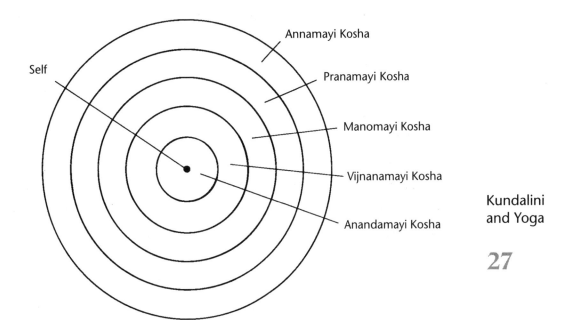

Self

Annamayi Kosha

Pranamayi Kosha

Manomayi Kosha

Vijnanamayi Kosha

Anandamayi Kosha

The five sheaths of consciousness

able to experience the bliss of *Anandamayi Kosha*. All the disturbances and turmoil of life are found within the other four *koshas*. The energy in these first four *koshas* is pranic. It supports both cellular and mental energy. Cellular energy undergoes changes and influences mental energy through the different *rasas*. Mental energy in turn influences the intellect and ego. When the ego gets tired of the ceaseless interplay of mental energy it requires rest. For normal human beings the cessation of mental energy is only possible in deep sleep. But sleep is not always able to be deep sleep; it is interrupted by dreams, and in dreams one's mental energy plays a major role. The only solution for total rest is to stop the mind. The mind depends on pranic energy for its activity. Thus controlling pranic energy and stopping *prana* is the only solution. Learning the techniques of working with *prana* is only possible in Yoga which is why the study of Yoga is so important.

In the dormant state of Kundalini, spiritual consciousness remains unmanifested and all of the creative principles are active. When Kundalini is aroused by Yoga aspirants, spiritual power and spiritual consciousness replace worldly consciousness and sense consciousness. Kundalini remains coiled as long as one's individual consciousness does not realize that there is a higher purpose in life and that there is another state of consciousness beyond the normal waking, sleeping, and dreaming states. That state may be glimpsed whenever one's desires for sensual enjoyments are fulfilled, whenever one finds no attraction in the phenomenal world, and one experiences a state of nonattachment, of introversion. The systematic withdrawal from indulgence opens doors to the inner world, and one experiences a light that leads towards the union that overcomes the duality of matter and mind. When this state of nonattachment becomes a permanent habit, the functions of individual consciousness completely stop and the aspirant becomes purified by the fire of detachment. One becomes calm and one-pointed. However, this state alone is not enough to change the nature of the Kundalini energy that is lying dormant. This latent energy can be activated by performing postures *(asanas)*, breath control *(pranayama)*, and gestures *(mudras)*, accompanied by meditation, mantra repetition, and visualization techniques. Then Kundalini becomes kinetic and adopts a course that is contrary to the law of gravitation, rising up and piercing through all the chakras located in the Sushumna.

The force that channels energy through the Sushumna in the spinal column comes from the fusion of the negative ions of *prana* with the positive ions of *apana*. *Apana* is the *prana* that exists in the region below the navel, the pelvic area. When *prana* and *apana* combine, the energy that is at rest in the base of the spine in its static form becomes active. If Kundalini is aroused before a proper inner environment has been created by *pranayama,* which cleanses the Nadis, the energy that rises in the Brahma Nadi comes back to its abode and coils again. This improper arousal may lead to what is called a "bad Kundalini experience."

It is therefore necessary to follow the eight steps prescribed by Yoga, referred to as *Ashtanga (asht* - eight, *ang* - limbs or parts) described in detail on pages 45–61. When the body is made quiescent by the practice of the eight steps, an unknown inner power is released that helps the body to keep an excellent state of physical health and vitality, and the mind to be quiet and free from fluctuations. In this state the mind exhibits better restraint when functioning at the sensory level. This restraint brings about a state of physical and mental motionlessness that allows the static coiled Kundalini energy to be activated and to move toward the highest place, the seventh chakra, described as the seat of cosmic consciousness in its Param Shiva form. Here again, a fusion between the negative and positive ions of *prana* and *apana* takes place, resulting in a great illumination. The ignorance of the mind, the primary cause of duality, is destroyed. One who experiences this state attains nondual consciousness and becomes enlightened.

According to Hindu scriptures, the true yogi—one who has achieved enlightenment—crosses the ocean of birth, disease, old age, and death. Hindu scriptures also state that it takes many lifetimes to become a true yogi. By the grace of a guru one may achieve this in one lifetime, but to gain a guru's grace is also not one lifetime's achievement. The evolution of consciousness is a gradual process and one has to spend many lifetimes in preparation. Achieving freedom from the desires for objects of the phenomenal world, which comes through non-attachment, takes time. The whole process of spiritual growth is made possible by *prana* and its carriers, the Nadis.

The Nadis

The word Nadi comes from the Sanskrit root *nad* meaning "movement." In the *Rigveda,* the most ancient Hindu scripture, the word *nadi* is used to mean "stream." The concept of Nadis is based on the understanding that they are channels; any channel through which anything flows is a Nadi. The *Shiva Purana* (4.40.5) clearly states that Nadis are not only nerves, but all kinds of channels. This is the reason that the Sanskrit term for nerve, *snayu,* is not used for Nadis in the texts of ancient Indian medicine, *Ayurveda*. There are two types of Nadis:

1. Subtle, non-material, invisible channels of subtle energy called Yoga Nadis. The subtle Nadis are again of two kinds: the channels of *manas* or the mind *(manovahini* or *manovahi nadis),* and the channels of *chitta,* the feeling self or being *(chittavahi nadis).*

2. Gross channels of subtle energy, visible as cords, vessels, or tubes. Included in this concept of Nadis are acupuncture meridians, nerves, muscles, and the streams of the cardiovascular and lymphatic systems, such as the arteries and veins.

Pranic energy is carried by Nadis that belong to each type, subtle and gross. The Nadis that carry pranic energy are known as *pranavahi* or *pranavahini nadis*. The gross *pranavahi nadis* work with the nerves of the central-, autonomic-, sympathetic-, and parasympathetic nervous systems. To some degree, these nerves, and the work and sense organs that are operated by them, are influenced by the Yoga Nadis such as Ida and Pingala, which are linked with the chakras. Thus the chakras work with Nadis of both kinds, gross and subtle, but Kundalini only works with the most subtle of the Nadis of the Sushumna. When Kundalini is awakened and *prana* is absorbed in Kundalini, the other Nadis stop functioning and the working of the chakras is temporarily suspended until the Kundalini becomes dormant again.

Ayurveda mentions 72,000 different Nadis. One's pulse is also called *nadi*, and medical diagnosis often commences by observing the throbbing of the *nadi* in the carotid artery. In the *Yoga Shikhopanishad* it is clearly stated that there are 101 Nadis that are connected to the Heart Center or Anahata Chakra. It continues: "The Ida Nadi is situated on the left side and the Pingala Nadi on the right side; between these two is the main Nadi, the Sushumna. Within the Sushumna is concealed the Brahma Nadi, which is pure in character like the supreme consciousness *(brahman)*. The Brahma Nadi is the void that connects to the Brahma Randhra, a void between the twin hemispheres of the brain, located in the uppermost chakra, the Sahasrara, the Thousand-petaled Lotus. One who knows this is the knower of the *Veda*."

Aspirants who are able to master the Nadis can attain the highest states of consciousness and gain the powers known as *siddhis* (perfections), giving them full command over the elements and *gunas*. The tantric treatise *Shiva Samhita* identifies fourteen principal Nadis. Of these, three main Nadis—Ida, Pingala, and Sushumna—are considered the most important for aspirants of Yoga and tantric practitioners. They are identified with the three main rivers of India: Ida is also known as Ganga, Pingala as Yamuna, and Sushumna as Saraswati. All three of these Nadis originate in the same region, the *kanda,* the fibrous material below the Muladhara Chakra around which nerves interweave. This junction of these three holy streams is called *yukta triveni (yukta* - combined, *triveni* - three streams). It takes the form of a downward-pointing bow or triangle in the center of which the Kundalini is coiled. The left side of the triangle is the Ida Nadi, the right side the Pingala Nadi, and the top the Sushumna Nadi. The three Nadis proceed upward from the Muladhara Chakra, with the Ida and Pingala alternating from the right to left sides of the Sushumna at each succeeding chakra, until they reach the Ajna Chakra, the point between the eyebrows, where they meet again, forming a gentle knot. The Ida and Pingala Nadis terminate in the left and right nostrils respectively and the Sushumna continues upward to the Sahasrara Chakra at the crown of the head. The meeting of these three streams in the Ajna Chakra is called *mukta triveni*. A yogi who has passed through the Vishuddha Chakra at the throat to the Ajna Chakra transcends the five elements and becomes freed *(mukta)* from the bondage of time-bound consciousness. That is why this meeting of the three Nadis is called the *mukta triveni*. The scriptures say: *triveni yoga sah prokta, tantra snanam maha phalam,* "this union is called *triveni,* and one who bathes in this *triveni* achieves great merit."

The fourteen major Nadis identified in the *Shiva Samhita* are:

1. Sushumna

The Sushumna is centrally situated and is the only Nadi that passes through the *meru danda* (spinal column). Certain studies of anatomy contradict the description of the Sushumna given by the tantric scriptures, stating that the central canal contains only cerebrospinal fluid, no nerve fibers, and that it is impossible neurologically for the spinal cord to have an opening at the top of the head for the inflow and outflow of *prana*. It is therefore difficult to provide an accurate anatomy of chakras.

According to the *Shiva Samhita, Yoga Shikhopanishad,* and many other tantric scriptures, the Sushumna originates in the Muladhara Chakra, pierces the *talu* (the palate at the base of the skull), and terminates in the Sahasrara Chakra at the crown of the head. Before it reaches the Ajna Chakra (situated in alignment with the eyebrows), the Sushumna Nadi divides into two branches: anterior and posterior. The anterior branch goes to the Ajna Chakra before reaching the Brahma Randhra, also known as *Bhramara Gupha (gupha* - cave, *bhramara* - bumble bee) or *Andha Kupa (andha* - blind, *kupa* - well), the seat of supreme consciousness. The posterior branch passes from behind the skull before it arrives at the Brahma Randhra.

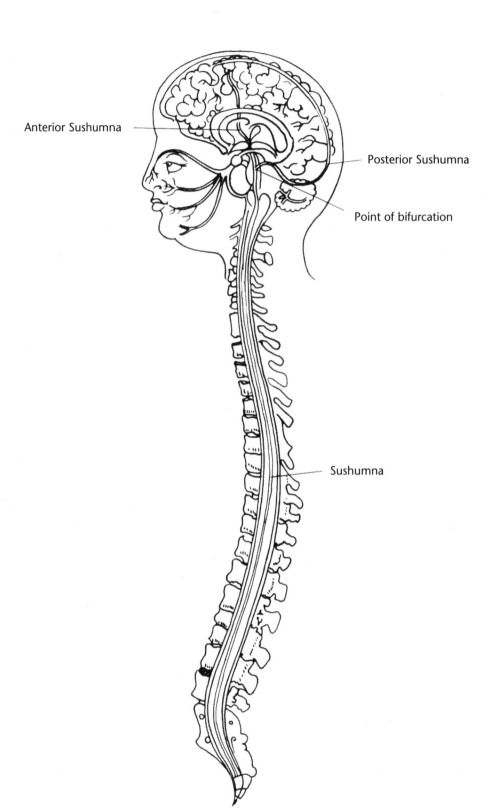

Anterior Sushumna

Posterior Sushumna

Point of bifurcation

Sushumna

Origin and termination of the Sushumna

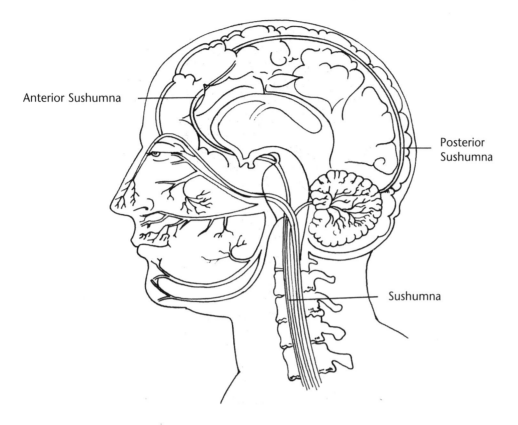

Anterior Sushumna

Posterior Sushumna

Sushumna

Bifurcation of the Sushumna

According to *Lalita Sahasranama* (a tantric text devoted to the Divine Mother), the Sushumna is not one Nadi but is made up of three principal Yoga Nadis, which are the subtlest of the subtle. The outermost part of the Sushumna is the fiery red Sushumna, which is beyond the limits of time. Inside it is the lustrous Vajra Nadi, also known as Vajrini, which is of the nature of the sun and of poison. Inside the Vajra Nadi is the pale Chitra Nadi, also known as Chitrini, which is of the nature of the moon and nectar-dropping. Inside the Chitrini Nadi is a void called the Brahma Nadi, which connects to the Brahma Randhra. The Sushumna and the void are both of the nature of inertia *(tamas)* whereas Vajrini is active *(rajas)* and Chitrini is pure illumination *(sattva)*. Chitrini radiates life energy; it is extremely subtle, pure intelligence and is revealed through Yoga to yogis (according to the *Kshata Chakra Nirupana,* verse 2). The Chitrini Nadi is responsible for dreams, hallucinations, and visions and is automatically active in painters, poets, and visionaries. (In Sanskrit, *chitra* means a handmade picture or a painting.) The terminating point of Chitrini Nadi is called Brahma Dvara, the door of *brahman,* through which Kundalini ascends to her final abode in the Soma Chakra within the Sahasrara Chakra.

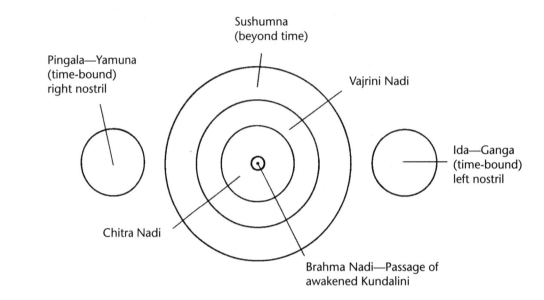

Cross section of the Sushumna according to Lalita Sahasranama

The Sushumna generally remains dormant when the other Nadis flow strongly and is activated when the flow through the other Nadis is restrained. The oscillating force of *prana* is responsible for breathing, causing most breaths taken in any given hour to be drawn in through only one nostril, thus activating either the Ida or the Pingala Nadis, and through them, the other Nadis. The Sushumna Nadi is activated only when the breath comes through both nostrils simultaneously, which typically happens only ten breaths per hour, at the change over from one nostril to the other. Through the yogic practice of *pranayama* (conscious breath control), the Sushumna can also be activated, though in this way, it causes a temporary suspension of inhalation and exhalation. The other Nadis then stop functioning and Kundalini is aroused to rise upward in the Sushumna through the Brahma Nadi. When the spiritual energy of Kundalini ascends in the

Sushumna it harmonizes the energy of the Ida and Pingala Nadis, which encircle the various chakras.

The Sushumna is the only Nadi that is not time-bound. A yogi who has established himself or herself in meditation at the Ajna Chakra (the midpoint between the eyebrows), in whom the spiritual energy of Kundalini has risen into the Brahma Randhra region, becomes a knower of the past, present, and future, *trikaladarshi* (*tri* - three, *kala* - time, *darshi* - seer). The yogi goes beyond time *(kala)* and cannot be touched by death (death is also called *kala* in Sanskrit). When breathing becomes suspended through *pranayama,* the functions of the physical body come to a standstill and the process of aging is stopped.

In addition to its brief operation each hour at each change of the nasal cycle, the Sushumna automatically operates at dawn and dusk. It has the effect of calming down the system, thus making meditation easy. That is one of the main

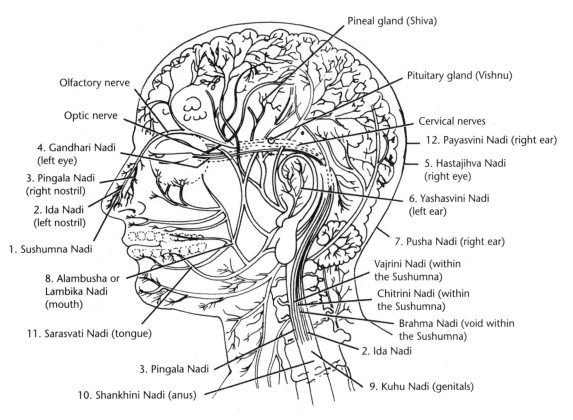

Major Nadis in the head

reasons that meditation at dawn and dusk has been incorporated in the religious practices of many traditions. Also, just before death all human beings breathe Sushumna breath, both nostrils working simultaneously. It is said that death—with the exception of accidental death—is not possible when either the Ida or Pingala Nadi alone is dominant. That is, death does not occur when one's breath is predominantly in only the left or the right nostril.

In acupuncture there is a meridian called the Governor Vessel Meridian, which has some correspondence with the Sushumna. In this meridian the energy flow starts at the tip of the coccyx, ascends the spine, reaches a point at the top of the head, and then courses down along the meridian line to a point just below the navel. In general, the acupuncture meridians may be equated with the Nadis that carry pranic energy.

2. Ida

The Ida Nadi is white in color. It starts and ends to the left of the Sushumna and is therefore considered part of the left channel of the Nadi system. It is the carrier of lunar energy currents. Yogis identify Ida as being a carrier of pranic energy *(pranavahini)* and claim it to be one of the most important mental *(manovahi)* Nadis. The *Gandharva Tantra* (ch. 5) says that the Ida Nadi is in the form of the moon so it conserves energy in the body and restores calmness to the mind. Ida is feminine in nature and is the storehouse of life-producing, maternal energy. As it nourishes and purifies the body and mind, it is called Ganga (the river Ganges) in tantric scriptures. In the depiction of the Supreme Self as a cosmic person *(Kala* or *Virat Purusha)* it is shown as the left eye. Like the Sushumna Nadi, the Ida Nadi originates in the *kanda,* the region below the Muladhara Chakra, but it is also connected with the left testicle in males. The Ida Nadi terminates in the left nostril. In Svara Yoga it represents the left breath, that is, breath flowing in and out of the left nostril. "Left" in Tantra is described as magnetic, female, visual, and emotional in nature. All of the yogic breathing practices of *pranayama* commence with inhalation through the left nostril which activates Ida Nadi, with the exception of *surya bhedan pranayama* (breathing to increase one's solar power). Aspirants of Yoga are advised to meditate when the Sushumna Nadi is working. If the Sushumna is not working, they are advised to meditate when Ida is operating, that is, when breath is flowing through the left nostril. The *Shiva Svarodaya* and the *Jnana Svarodaya* recommend that all important activities, especially those that give stability to life, are best done when the Ida Nadi is active.

In the system of Svara Yoga, practitioners observe the custom of keeping the left nostril open during the day so that its *sattvik* lunar energy will balance the *rajasik* solar energy that is received during the daylight hours. By creating a balance in oneself, one becomes more relaxed and more alert mentally. The Ida Nadi is responsible for restoring energy to the brain. Ida is situated on the left side of the spinal column *(meru danda)* and has been wrongly identified as the chain of nerve ganglia connected with nerve fibers called the sympathetic cord. A close similarity exists, because the sympathetic system controls and influences respiration, and because respiration is connected with the nostrils. However, Ida is neither a nerve nor a sympathetic cord; it is a mental channel, a *manovahi nadi*. Locating this Nadi with modern technical devices has thus far not proved possible, but the *pranavahi* aspect of Ida can clearly be felt through the effects of practicing the science of breath *(svara sadhana)* and *pranayama*.

Folklore from around the world, and especially in India, relates the moon to the psyche. In the *Purusha Sukta* it is said: "The moon was born from the *manas* of the *Virata Purusha* (Supreme Self)" *(chandrama manaso jatah)*. During the ascending moon cycle (from the new moon to the full moon), Ida is dominant for nine days in a fortnight at the time of sunrise and sunset.

3. Pingala

The Pingala Nadi is part of the right channel, the carrier of solar energy currents. Like the sun, the Pingala is masculine in nature. It is a storehouse of energy that, according to the *Vishvasara Tantra,* is consumed in muscular activities requiring physical strength and speed. The Pingala Nadi makes the physical body more dynamic and more efficient, and it is this Nadi that provides added vitality and male power. Unlike Ida's calming, mentally focusing, *sattvik* lunar energy, Pingala's *rajasik* solar energy causes diversification of the mind and it is therefore not suitable for meditation. Like the Ida, the Pingala is also purifying, but its cleansing is like fire. Concentration on the sun by doing the yogic exercise of *Surya Namaskar* at sunrise helps to turn the untamed masculine energy of Pingala into constructive energy *(Vishvasara Tantra)*. As Ida is identified with the Ganges, Pingala is identified with the Yamuna river.

Pingala is sometimes represented as the right eye. In Svara Yoga, the Pingala represents the right breath, that is, breath flowing in and out of the right nostril. In Tantra "right" is described as electrical, male, verbal, and rational in nature. All of the yogic breathing practices of *pranayama* commence with inhalation through the left nostril, except *surya bhedana pranayama* (breathing to increase solar power) in which inhalation begins through the right nostril, thus exciting Pingala Nadi. This *pranayama* is performed to increase vigor, stamina, and solar energy. In Svara Yoga it is acknowledged that Pingala Nadi makes a male "pure male," just as Ida makes a female "pure female." Right nostril dominance is recommended for physical activities, temporary jobs, discussions, debates, and, indeed, duels.

The *Purusha Sukta* says: "From the eyes comes the sun" *(chakshore suryo ajayatah),* meaning that the sun was born from the eyes of the *Virata Purusha.* The eyes are vehicles of the sun. The eyes discriminate. The eyes and the sun are related to the intellect and the rational brain. The night is a time for fantasy, and dominance of the rational brain (right-nostril dominance) at night prevents one from burning off energy through fantasizing. Great thinkers use the night for contemplation. It is said that "when it is night for worldly people, it is day for yogis." The yogic practice of keeping the right nostril open at night, when solar energy is less strong, maintains the balance of a healthy organism. Keeping the *sattvik* Ida Nadi active during the day and the *rajasik* Pingala Nadi active at night *(tamasik)* increases one's overall vitality and longevity.

The Pingala, like the Ida, is a mental *(manovahi)* and pranic *(pranavahi)* Nadi. It is more active during the descending moon cycle (from full moon to new moon) and operates for nine days in a fortnight at the time of sunrise and sunset. Willful control over the Ida and Pingala Nadis can be achieved through the practice of Svara Yoga or the disciplines of *pranayama.* The Pingala Nadi brings energy down from the center of combustion of the brain where matter (oxygen and glucose) is converted into life-giving energy *(prana).*

4. Gandhari

The Gandhari Nadi stretches from below the corner of the left eye to the big toe of the left foot. Gandhari is situated by the side of Ida Nadi and helps support it. It is used to carry psychic energy from the lower part of the body upward to the Ajna Chakra. The Gandhari Nadi is energized by practicing the form of the lotus posture called *baddha padmasana,* in which the practitioner crosses the arms behind the back while sitting in the lotus posture and then grasps the big toe of the left foot with the right hand and the big toe of the right foot with the left hand.

5. Hastajihva

The Hastajihva Nadi stretches from below the corner of the right eye to the big toe of the left foot. Along with the Gandhari Nadi, it is a complementary Nadi to Ida; the three together form the left channel. The *Shiva Svarodaya* describes the termination point of Hastajihva as being in the right eye, although the *Jabal Upanishad* (named after Satyakama Jabal) maintains that the termination point is in the left eye.

6. Yashasvini

The Yashasvini Nadi stretches from the right big toe to the left ear and is a complementary Nadi to the Pingala Nadi.

7. Pusha

The Pusha Nadi stretches from the left big toe to the right ear. This Nadi, along with the Yashasvini and Pingala Nadis, forms the right channel.

8. Alambusha

The Alambusha Nadi begins at the anus and terminates in the mouth.

9. Kuhu

The Kuhu Nadi originates in the throat and terminates in the genitals. Kuhu Nadi helps Chitrini Nadi to serve as carrier of the *bindu* (the semen or essence of the seminal fluid); together they cause ejaculation. Practitioners of an exercise known as *vajrauli* are able to master this Nadi and raise their seminal fluid from the second chakra to the Soma Chakra within the Sahasrara Chakra. The practice of *vajrauli* is for the male aspirant. He begins by sucking water up through the *lingam* (male genital organ). Milk is gradually mixed with the water in increasing proportions. Once the aspirant is able to suck pure milk, he may advance to the stage where he is able to absorb oil, which is heavier than milk. The next step is mastery over the ingestion of pure mercury. During these processes the aspirant develops his potential to work with *prana,* and when he advances to the point where he can suck mercury through his *lingam,* he will then be able to draw in his own seminal fluid, along with the vaginal fluid from his female counterpart. This ultimate practice brings him into a state of *samadhi* (realized nonduality) through the union of opposites (the two fluids) inside his own physical body.

Exercises of this kind should only be practiced under the guidance of an experienced teacher!

10. Shankhini

Shankhini originates in the throat and moves between the Sarasvati and Gandhari Nadis on the left side of the Sushumna Nadi, terminating in the anus. Shankhini Nadi becomes active through the purificatory practices of *vasti* (enemas) and *Ganesha Kriya* (rinsing the anus). These two practices have great medicinal value; they should be learned through the instruction of a Yoga teacher adept in them.

11. Sarasvati Nadi

Along with the Ida, Pingala, and Sushumna Nadis, the Sarasvati Nadi originates in the *kanda* of the Muladhara Chakra and terminates in the tongue. In India it is a common saying that Sarasvati, the goddess of speech, knowledge, and the fine arts, lives on the tongue, and that once a day she expresses herself in all human beings; whatever one says at that time becomes true. By observance of disciplines and purification, this Nadi becomes active and eventually whatever one says during that time will come true. The end of the tongue is in the throat, and therefore it is sometimes said that Sarasvati resides in the throat, in particular, the vocal cords, the physical organ of speech. Sarasvati Nadi is camphor white in color and lunar in nature; it runs parallel to the Sushumna and is a complementary channel.

12. Payasvini Nadi

The Payasvini Nadi flows between the Pusha and Sarasvati Nadis. Its termination point is located in the right ear. Ancient iconography depicts deities, sages, and incarnations of the divine Self *(avataras)* as wearing spectacular earrings. These ornaments served a special purpose. A certain part of the earlobe is connected with the cranial nerves and a pure metal earring inserted at this point gives the system access to ions and static electricity from the environment. Thus yogis, by piercing the ears and inserting earrings, are able to activate the Payasvini Nadi. Even today, tantrics known as Kanphata yogis (belonging to the Nath sect of yogis) wear large hooped earrings.

13. Varuni Nadi

The Varuni Nadi is situated between the Yashasvini and Kuhu Nadis. It is a *pranavahi* Nadi that helps to purify the toxins in the lower trunk area. Like the Shankhini Nadi, this Nadi terminates in the anus and can be activated by *vasti* (enemas) and *Ganesha Kriya* (rinsing the anus). This Nadi can also be activated through water purification. When Varuni Nadi is not flowing properly, *apana* (the wind or air that resides in the lower trunk) can become disturbed, causing an increase in *tamas* (inertia). Varuni Nadi pervades the whole area of the lower torso and assists in keeping *apana* free of toxins. *Apana* and Varuni Nadi together help in the process of excretion.

14. Vishvodara

The Vishvodara Nadi flows between the Kuhu and Hastajihva Nadis and resides in the area of the naval. This Nadi is connected with the digestion of all kinds of food. The Vishvodara Nadi can be energized by the yogic exercises *nauli kriya* and Uddiyana Bandha (detailed later in this chapter), which involve contracting the rectal/abdominal muscles. Vishvodara Nadi is related to the adrenal glands and the pancreas and, together with Varuni Nadi, improves the distribution and flow of *prana* throughout the body, especially the *prana* that rises through the Sushumna Nadi.

The scriptures on Yoga mention many other minor Nadis such as: the Raka Nadi, which causes thirst, sneezing, and phlegm in the nostrils; the Shura Nadi, which terminates between the eyebrows; the Wilambini Nadi, which originates in the *kanda* and ramifies upward, downward, and obliquely. However, the above-mentioned fourteen Nadis are the major ones. Of these, the first ten are the most important because they are related to what are called the ten "gates" through which *prana* leaves the body. According to Hindu tradition, the body is a castle with ten openings or gates and, at death, one's vital force exits from one of the ten. The *Shiva Svarodaya* connects the first ten Nadis with the ten gates as follows:

1. Sushumna, connected with Brahma Randhra, the tenth gate (fontanel)

2. Ida, the left nostril, connected with the ninth gate

3. Pingala, the right nostril, connected with the eighth gate

4. Gandhari, the left eye, connected with the seventh gate

5. Hastajihva, the right eye, connected with the sixth gate

6. Yashasvina, the left ear, connected with the fifth gate

7. Pusha, the right ear, connected with the fourth gate

8. Alambusha, the mouth, connected with the third gate

9. Kuhu, the genitals, connected with the second gate

10. Shankhini, the anus, connected with the first gate

Most animals leave the body through the first and second gates: they defecate and urinate at the time of death. Most humans leave the body through one of the third to ninth gates, dying with open mouth, bleeding nostrils, open eyes, or droplets of blood coming out the ears. Only yogis leave the body from the tenth gate, the gate of liberation *(moksha)*. This gate is open at the time of birth and is felt as the "soft spot" in a newborn baby's head. After six months it begins to harden, after which it can only be reopened through special yogic practices. One who leaves the body from this gate does not come back and is free from the cycle of life and death.

HOW TO AWAKEN KUNDALINI

The primary prerequisite for awakening the sleeping energy of Kundalini is purification of the body and the mind. Purification is a device to free the entire system of accumulated toxins. Because the body and the mind always work in coordination with each other, purification of the body helps that of the mind, and vice versa.

Purification of the Body

There are many ways in which the body can be deeply cleansed. Some devices are common to many different cultures; various medical sciences have their own methods. Ayurveda, the Indian science of medicine, prescribes fasting as the most effective method. Three days of taking only lukewarm water cleanses the body of toxins and cures disorders without medicines. Hatha Yoga presents a well-defined system known as *Kshata Karmas,* six acts of purification (*kshata* - six, *karma* - act). These were devised by yogis to purify the body and mind simultaneously. When properly guided and administered, these six acts of purification are very effective. They are best performed in a clean, quiet place, and it is strongly recommended that they be done under the guidance of an adept master of these acts. Yogis advise that the specifics of the *Kshata Karma* techniques should be kept secret among yogic initiates. The *Kshata Karmas* are:

1. *Dhauti* – Throat Cleansing

Take a strip of natural cotton cloth, four finger breadths wide and fifteen spans long. (One span equals the length of the hand from the forefinger to the wrist. Individual span measurement differs from person to person; one thus uses one's own measuring span in these exercises.) A long strip of soft, new, muslin cloth would serve well. Wet it with warm water, swallow it slowly, and then draw it out slowly and gently, according to the instructions of the master. Begin by swallowing one span the first day, and increase daily by one span in length. Make sure the cloth is warm when swallowing it.

The *dhauti* practice takes fifteen days. Persons suffering from diseases caused by phlegm may extend the practice. *Dhauti* cleans the alimentary canal, cures bronchial diseases, asthma, diseases of the spleen, skin diseases, and all diseases caused by phlegm.

2. *Vasti* – Anal/Lower Intestinal Tract Cleansing

Take a piece of smooth, fresh bamboo about six finger breadths long and about one and one-half finger breadths in diameter. Apply some butter to make it smooth. Sit in a bathtub with water reaching the navel. Assume *utkatasana* (sit on the haunches, balancing the body on the toes) and insert the tube about four finger breadths into the anus; contract the anus to draw in water. Shake the water internally and then expel it. Repeat many times.

3. *Neti* – Nasal/Sinus Cleansing

Take a piece of thread that is free of any knots. Smooth it with *ghee* (clarified butter). Place one end of the thread into one nostril and, closing the other nostril with one finger, inhale through the open nostril and exhale through the mouth. By repeating this process the thread will be inhaled into the throat. Gently pull the thread. Repeat the process, beginning with the opposite nostril. Then it will be possible to place the thread in one nostril and draw it out through the other. Thus the process is complete.

Neti purifies the nasal passages, the sinuses, the frontal lobe, and the front part of the skull. It stimulates the whole nervous system, increases vision, and enables one to perceive subtle things with the eyes. *Neti* is also performed by drinking water up through the nostrils and spitting it out through the mouth. This is called *jala neti*.

4. *Trataka* – Eye-Cleansing Exercise

Trataka is a yogic practice of gazing with fixed eyes on a minute object with complete concentration and without blinking until tearing occurs. When the tears flow, the eyes are closed and the after-image is visualized until it vanishes.

Through *trataka* one achieves one-pointedness of the mind. *Trataka* helps cure diseases of the eyes and enhances growth and development of the pineal gland. It also develops "witness consciousness," a state of watching one's internal and external actions without emotional involvement.

5. *Nauli* – Abdominal Exercise

This exercise is the crown of Hatha Yoga. It is difficult and requires much practice. In the beginning it may seem impossible, but through constant willpower *nauli* can be mastered.

Leaning slightly forward, stand with feet apart and the hands resting on the knees. Expel all the air from the lungs. Contract the abdominal muscles, pulling them up inside as much as possible. Two Nadis will show prominence. Rotate them with the abdominal muscles to the right and to the left with the speed of a fast-circling eddy. Breathe in after the rotation. Repeat several times.

Nauli stimulates the gastric fire, increases digestive power, induces joy, increases skin glow, stimulates the nervous system, and balances disorders created by wind, bile, and mucus.

6. *Kapalabhati* – Bellows-Breathing Exercise

Breathe in and out quickly and uniformly, like the bellows of a blacksmith. Stop as soon as any strain is felt. *Kapalabhati* destroys all diseases caused by phlegm.

There is another, separate purification exercise called *gaja karni* that is not part of the *Kshata Karmas* but that is also prescribed in Hatha Yoga. It is performed by drawing *apana* up to the throat and vomiting any substances (food, water, etc.) that are present in the stomach. The gradual practice of this stomach cleansing brings the breath and all of the Nadis under control.

PURIFICATION OF THE MIND

The mind is not an entity in itself; it is only a tool of the I-consciousness. Experience of the world outside is easily made possible by the tools that the I-consciousness has, but to experience the world within, the I-consciousness needs to become free from the impressions of the outside world, which is difficult. It is not possible in waking consciousness, dream, or deep sleep. It is possible only when the mind is calm.

To purify the mind, all branches and schools of Yoga prescribed an eight part formula, known as *Ashtanga Yoga* (*asht* - eight, *ang* - limbs or parts, *yoga* - union with the true Self). The eight limbs are: (1) *Yama* (Control), (2) *Niyama* (Golden Rules of Conduct), (3) *Asana* (Postures), (4) *Pranayama* (Control of Breath), (5) *Pratyahara* (Withdrawal of Sensory Perceptions), (6) *Dharana* (Concentration), (7) *Dhyana* (Uninterrupted Meditation), (8) *Samadhi* (Uninterrupted *Dhyana*, Complete Equilibrium). The practice of Ashtanga Yoga is necessary, no matter which yogic path is followed. Only by practicing these eight steps of Yoga can one experience true freedom from time-bound consciousness. (For further background on Yoga, please refer to the appendix.)

The ancient seers of Yoga believed that the ultimate goal of human life is self-realization: living a life that is not centered around the gratification of senses, but one in which energy is used in the right proportion in every field of life. The ancient seers believed that one has to live a disciplined life and that an organized and systematic life is the beginning of all Yoga. For them, Yoga was not a hobby, but a way of living as a wise person. Each of the eight steps of Ashtanga Yoga was designed to create a selfless person. Humans tend to be selfish, which makes them not only unfriendly to those around them but also to the environment in which they live. Yoga teachers therefore advise their aspirants to follow a code of conduct to help them accomplish the eight steps of purifying the mind, controlling the unnecessary expenditure of energy through living a disciplined life.

1. Eat less. Eat simple, nourishing, fresh, easily digestible food. Eat to satisfy hunger, but entertain no lethargy; remain light, alert, and joyful.

2. Drink less. But not less than the minimum requirement of the body, according to age and seasonal conditions.

3. Talk less. Avoid unnecessary discussions, lies, and fantasies.

4. Sleep less. Avoid the consumption of energy in dreams.

5. Stay alone. For some time enjoy your own self. Avoid the excitement that comes when one is surrounded by people.

6. Avoid the excessive use of sour, sharp, and pungent tastes.

7. Avoid excessive intimacy or friendship and extreme hatred.

8. Be detached from worldly accomplishments and acquisitions.

9.   Be strong, mentally and physically. Be unshakable by success and failure.

10. Have a restricted mind and don't run after everything that fascinates you.

11. Do not spend energy in the gratification of sensual desires.

12. Keep a distance from members of the opposite sex. Avoid getting massages from them. Massage yourself, but don't massage to enjoy touch.

13. Avoid all kinds of aromas, smells, and oils; use natural-smelling flowers and incense.

14. Be independent; don't depend on others; do your things yourself.

15. Serve those from whom you learn (your guru).

16. Give up desires that satisfy only you.

17. Give up anger. It destroys the electro-chemical balance.

18. Give up pride, self-esteem, and egotism.

19. Give up greed. It makes one selfish, suspicious, jealous, and cunning.

20. Survive on the minimum requirement.

21. Don't deceive anybody. It creates a double personality and causes a person to lose self-confidence and personal magnetism *(ojas)*.

22. Don't boast. It increases egotism.

23. Don't speak lies. They only show that you do not trust yourself.

24. Don't worship ghosts and spirits; worship divinity in pure, compassionate, living form.

25. Don't use drugs to prolong life. They destroy the natural endurance.

26. Avoid going to conferences, public gatherings, theaters, and places where the mind gets excited.

27. Be content. It gives satisfaction.

28. Be thoughtful, but do not wait for someone to thank you.

Following these twenty-eight suggestions helps aspirants to overcome their worldly nature, which makes them forget their innermost being. When people are completely materialistic and external-minded, they are under the sway of traits such as sensuality, greed, lust, wickedness, pride, and anger. However, if one follows these twenty-eight practical suggestions, the pain and intense suffering that is a natural outcome of worldly living will never come. This code of conduct also creates an attitude in the aspirant that makes it easy to follow the path of Ashtanga Yoga. After one has practiced these twenty-eight disciplines, one is ready to undertake the eight steps that lead to the ultimate union of the I-consciousness with the supreme consciousness.

1. *Yama* – Control

Yama is a process by which the actions of the body and the functions of the mind are volitionally restrained. It purifies one's words, thoughts, and deeds, enabling the aspirant to reach the deeper aspect of his or her own self that remains dormant in an undisciplined life. Through the practice of *yama,* an unknown inner power is experienced, because the body becomes quiescent and the mind becomes tranquil and able to function better. There are ten *yamas:*

1. Non-violence
2. Truth
3. Honesty
4. Sexual continence
5. Forbearance
6. Fortitude
7. Kindness
8. Straight-forwardness
9. Moderation in diet
10. Purity (bodily cleansing)

2. *Niyama* – Golden Rules of Conduct

After following the *yamas* one will be able to follow effortlessly the rules of conduct, thus enhancing the development of one's spiritual nature that makes one harmless, selfless, friendly, loving, and respectful to all creation, from mineral to man. The ten *niyamas* are:

1. Austerity

2. Contentment

3. Belief in God

4. Charity

5. Worship of God in any form

6. Openness and constant study by reading or listening to explanations of teachings or doctrines and scriptures

7. Modesty

8. Having a discerning mind

9. Repetition of prayers *(japa)*

10. Observance of vows and performing sacrifices

The constant practice of *niyamas* creates a spiritual attitude and awakens one's "witness consciousness." One becomes reflective and modest, and one's spiritual energy starts working. Through application of these disciplines the mind is automatically weaned from unnecessary attachment to worldly objects, and one is able to concentrate.

3. *Asana* – Postures (literally, "seated postures")

If the body is not under control, then the mind cannot work unobstructed. Thus our own body is our greatest obstacle. To quiet the mind we must practice some special techniques to achieve control over our musculature and limbs to make them feel easy without any movement. A motionless body makes the mind quiet. This technique of making the body feel comfortable and motionless volitionally is called *asana*.

Asanas are designed to provide more elasticity to musculature, to regulate circulation, to direct energy to move at will, and to relax the body. The muscles sometimes present obstacles and then the mind can't become calm. Those who live a pure, disciplined life, however, will not be bothered by this body consciousness and will be able to select a posture suitable for concentration. There are eighty-four postures described in Hatha Yoga, but not all postures are pre-scribed at all times and in all situations. There are postures which are used for meditation, for controlling the breath, and for the practice of *mantra japa* (sound repetition). In these postures, the rate of breathing changes, becoming slow and deep. There are also postures that increase the power of endurance in the body. By practicing various postures, the body is cleansed of toxins and is made a more suitable tool.

The most important features of *asanas* are that the spine is kept straight, the head and neck are erect and in alignment, and the body is comfortably motion-less. Achieving the correct posture has an equalizing effect, stilling the forces present in the body and slowing the breath rate and blood circulation; it makes one firm and steady, it facilitates meditation, and it helps to cure diseases and fickleness of the mind. Some *asanas* activate various nerve centers and help the body to secrete growth hormones and produce antibodies. The *Shandilyopanishad* says that all sicknesses of the body are destroyed by practicing postures *(asanas),* and even poisons can be assimilated.

One (any one) *asana* should be selected and mastered if it is not possible for one to master all eighty-four of them. In the *Mandalabrahmanopanishad* it is said that when a posture is executed properly there is a natural feeling of ease and comfort when a posture is assumed; and there is the ability to prolong the dura-tion of the posture without discomfort. Patanjali's *Yoga Sutra* recommends any posture in which one can stay for a long period of time without any discomfort or feeling of uneasiness. *Padmasana* (lotus posture) and *siddhasana* ("accomplished" posture) are two highly praised *asanas.*

Tantra believes that when an aspirant can stay in one *asana* for about six hours, he or she develops a power called *asana siddhi.* One's personal magne-tism increases and whatever is needed comes without being sought after. The *Trishikhibrahmanopanishad* says that the three worlds are conquered by one who has mastered *asanas.*

Patanjali offers two suggestions for acquiring mastery of *asanas:* (1) hold the physical posture in an immovable position for long periods, gradually mastering the posture through will power, and (2) meditate on the infinite lord who holds and balances the earth as the great serpent Shesha. When the aspirant is able to sit in one posture steadily and comfortably for a long time, there is a movement of energy in higher centers. Through the steadiness of the *asana* the mind becomes steady.

4. *Pranayama* – Breath Control

Through *prana,* the vital life force, the body works as a living organism. *Prana* connects living beings with their environment and provides all kinds of energy necessary for their survival. Because we human beings receive this vital life force from breathing in, *pranayama* is control of the breath. The nervous system is especially related to *prana;* control of the breath is possible only with the help of the nerves. Slow and deep breathing is not the same as *pranayama,* although it does promote health to a reasonable extent, due to the increased intake of oxygen in a slower rhythm than the normal rate of fifteen breaths per minute. Slowing down the rhythm of breathing slows down the rhythm of the mind, which makes the mind calm, but this is not *pranayama.* It is just slow breathing. (The benefits of reducing the rate of breath are mentioned in my book, *Breath, Mind, and Consciousness,* p. 51.)

Pranayama is breathing in a special way, in which *prana* is controlled and the suspension of the breath can be increased. Both inhaling and exhaling are done through the nostrils. Nasal breathing influences the frontal lobe of the brain because inhalation of air, which is cold by nature, cools the frontal sinuses and, therefore, the frontal lobe. The change of temperature influences the brain activity; the mind, which uses the brain as a tool, also becomes calm. An oscillating state of mind is created by breathing through the nostrils, which activates the Ida and Pingala Nadis. Suspension of the breath creates a non-oscillating state in the mind. When breathing through the nostrils ceases, the Ida and Pingala function much less, and the flow in the Sushumna starts. Stopping the breath with the help of the nerves decreases muscular activity; when *pranayama* is done while in an *asana* that makes the body still, it creates prolonged and deep concentration. Cognition, conation, and affection work as long as one breathes. Slowing down the breath slows down these functions, and stopping the breath stops them.

The object of *pranayama* is to achieve the state of *kevali kumbhaka,* automatic breath suspension. To achieve this state, the aspirant has to follow the twenty-eight code-of-conduct suggestions mentioned earlier. One who sleeps less but deeply, eats less but has a nourishing diet, has no longings or worldly desires, and has a strong desire to achieve the state of *turiya,* should practice *pranayama* in a private place under the guidance of a efficient and kind guru. Morning (dawn) and evening (dusk) are the best times to practice *pranayama.*

The process of *pranayama* consists of three steps:

1. Inhalation *(puraka)*

2. Holding the breath in the lungs or breath suspension *(kumbhaka)*

3. Exhalation *(rechaka)*

The breath is suspended *(kumbhaka)* both after inhalation *(puraka)* and after exhalation *(rechaka).* The suspension of breath between *puraka* and *rechaka* is called *antah* (internal) *kumbhaka,* because the lungs are holding the air which has been inhaled. The suspension of breath when the lungs are empty after exhalation and before the next intake of breath is called *vahya* (external) *kumbhaka.* In *puraka,* the breath is inhaled through one of the two nostrils (preferably the left nostril, except in special *pranayamas*), like sucking water through a tube. In *rechaka* the air is expelled through the alternate nostril to make the lungs empty.

During *pranayama* three kinds of muscular control *(bandhas)* should be adopted. *Bandhas* are devices to lock the areas in the body where energy is temporarily contained so that it may be directed in the way that the yogi desires. These three *bandhas* help to open the Sushumna path and awaken Kundalini.

1. Mula Bandha: This lock is performed by pressing the perineum with the left heel and placing the right foot upon the left thigh. The *sadhaka* (practitioner) should then contract the anus, drawing *apana* upward through the Sushumna. Pressing the anus with the heel, the *sadhaka* then forcibly compresses the air, repeating the process until *apana* moves further upward. When *apana* reaches the region of the navel, it increases the gastric fire. Then *apana,* combined with the fire of the Manipura Chakra, pierces through the Anahata Chakra, where it mixes with *prana* whose seat is in the region of the heart and lungs. *Prana* is hot in nature, and this heat further increases with the combustion created from the fusion of the negative ions of *prana* and the positive ions of *apana.* According to tantric scriptures, it is through this extreme heat and combustive force that the sleeping Kundalini is awakened, just as a serpent struck by a stick hisses and straightens itself. Then, like a snake entering its hole, Kundalini enters the Sushumna and ascends through the Brahma Nadi. Yogis therefore make Mula Bandha a regular practice.

2. Uddiyana Bandha: The literal meaning of *uddiyana* in Sanskrit is "flying up." The yogi performs this lock so that the great bird of *prana* will fly up through the Sushumna incessantly. The aspirant draws the abdominal muscles of the navel region back toward the spine and up toward the heart. This is facilitated by first expelling all the air present in the abdominal region. According to the *shastras* (scriptures), this *bandha* rejuvenates the body. It is called "the lion that kills the elephant of death." An aging *sadhaka* can become youthful through regular practice of Uddiyana Bandha. It takes about six months of regular practice to master the art of Uddiyana Bandha, after which *prana* begins to flow upward through the Sushumna, reaching the Sahasrara Chakra. This action brings about the last fusion in the Thousand-petaled Lotus, and at this point the *sadhaka* automatically achieves the state of *samadhi.*

3. Jalandhara Bandha: This *bandha* is performed by contracting the throat and then placing the chin firmly in the hollow spot between the chest and the neck (approximately eight finger breadths above the chest). There is a network of subtle Nadis at this juncture. The throat is the location of the Vishuddha Chakra, and it binds the sixteen supporting organs: toes, ankles, knees, thighs, perineum, reproductive organs, navel, heart, neck, throat/tongue, nose, center of eyebrows, forehead, head, cerebrum, and the Sushumna Nadi in the skull. Through the regular practice of Jalandhara Bandha, all diseases of the throat are destroyed and the sixteen supporting organs are vitalized.

The Jalandhara Bandha cuts off circulation of the fluids from the head, and an independent circuit is established. Through this *bandha* the downward flow of fluids from the cavity of the palate is arrested. This fluid is described as *soma* (nectar or elixir). This cerebrospinal fluid is composed of various nutrient hormones that enhance the growth and development of the organism. Normally this fluid flows downward and is burned away by the gastric fire. When complete mastery is gained over Jalandhara Bandha, the nectar does not flow downward, and the Ida and Pingala Nadis, which are lunar and solar currents, respectively, are constricted and cease to function. This slows down the rate of breath until it becomes motionless. The *soma* is recycled and channeled to revitalize the total organism. The practitioner is rejuvenated, diseases are removed, and the life span is lengthened.

The three *bandhas* are excellent devices for awakening Kundalini, opening the path of the Sushumna, stilling the activity of the Ida and Pingala, fusing *prana* with *apana,* and perfecting Kundalini Yoga. The locks should be used in the following manner: (1) the anal lock (Mula Bandha) should be done in the beginning and maintained throughout the *pranayama;* (2) at the end of inhalation *(puraka),* the chin lock (Jalandhara Bandha) should be performed; (3) at the end of exhalation *(rechaka),* abdominal retraction (Uddiyana Bandha) should be performed; (4) during breath suspension *(kumbhaka),* all three locks should be used.

The order of *pranayama* according to the *Trishikhibrahmanopanishad* is:

1. Exhalation *(rechaka)*

2. Inhalation *(puraka)*

3. Suspension or holding the breath in the lungs *(kumbhaka)*

4. Exhalation *(rechaka)*

5. Suspension again with empty lungs *(kumbhaka)*

To perform *pranayama,* one should assume a posture in which the body is erect, the upper and lower teeth are not touching, and the eyes are fixed on the point between the eyebrows. One should then perform the chin lock (Jalandhara Bandha). Then one should do the expiration to empty the lungs through the right nostril by blocking the left nostril with the fingers of the right hand.

After expiration one should block the right nostril and inhale through the left nostril, counting to sixteen. Then the breath should be held in the lungs to a count of sixty-four. Then one should exhale through the right nostril to a count of thirty-two. The relative measures of *puraka - kumbhaka - rechaka* should be 1 - 4 - 2. The *kumbhaka* discussed here is called *sahita kumbhaka (sahit -* together) because it is done together with *puraka* and *rechaka.*

Breathing alternately between the two nostrils affects the pranic currents, cleans the subtle pranic channels (Nadis), opens the Sushumna, cools the two hemispheres of the brain, suspends the activity of the brain and the mind, and temporarily stops any internal dialogue. There are many kinds of *pranayamas* with different measures of *puraka, rechaka,* and *kumbhaka*. Through the practice of breath control a non-respiratory state is gradually developed in which a natural cessation of breathing occurs *(kevali kumbhaka). Kevali kumbhaka* leads to deep concentration. The period of retention of breath must be prolonged gradually and cautiously until the breath is automatically suspended. After the aspirant becomes well versed in *pranayama,* the energy can be directed to the Sushumna to promote the rise of Kundalini Shakti through the Brahma Nadi.

Pranayama is much more effective in a body that has been purified by the *Kshata Karmas.* The neuro-motor function of breathing is linked with the limbic system of the brain, which is also connected with emotional behavior. Because of this connection, emotional changes change the breathing pattern. Yogic breathing sometimes brings out deeply buried emotions from the subconscious that transport the aspirant to different states of consciousness. In the first stage of *pranayama* the aspirant perspires, in the second stage the body shakes, and in the third stage the body becomes light and the yogi can levitate. These signs appear only after a long-term practice of *pranayama.* Accomplishment of *pranayama* brings joy, satisfaction, purity of mind, calmness, lightness of the eyes and skin, good digestion, self-confidence, and *siddhis* (attainments).

5. *Pratyahara* – Withdrawal of Sensory Perceptions

Pratyahara is withdrawal of the senses from the objects toward which they naturally flow. Thus all connections with the outside world are broken. *Pratyahara* appears to be the control of the senses with the mind, but the real technique is the withdrawal of the mind into the Self. It consists of two steps: (1) breath suspension *(kumbhaka)* and (2) holding of the mind. Normally, when we are completely absorbed in something, our sense organs do not register any signals coming from without. Thus our daily experience shows that withdrawal of the senses and the mind is possible. All that is needed is deep concentration, coupled with complete absorption.

Tantric *pratyahara* is practiced when the dormant Kundalini energy in the Muladhara Chakra is roused. *Prana* is absorbed in the mind, and the mind is absorbed in Kundalini. When Kundalini moves up through the chakras, the energies residing in the elements (in the first five chakras) are absorbed in the Kundalini. The senses work with the help of *prana,* so when *prana* is held in *kumbhaka* the function of the senses is automatically suspended. The sense organs connected with the chakras are also withdrawn and absorbed in Kundalini. This step-by-step absorption and withdrawal is *pratyahara.* The suspension of breath is essential in this practice because the Sushumna most often is in a dormant state. Breathing activates the Ida and Pingala Nadis, but it is the suspension of breath *(kumbhaka)* that activates the Sushumna, Vajrini, and Chitra Nadis.

The constant practice of *pratyahara* brings about the internalization and absorption of the mind. The senses become still and renounce their craving for objects. This practice affords the aspirant supreme mastery over the senses, making the next step, *dharana,* or deep concentration, easy.

6. *Dharana* – Concentration

According to the *Rudrayamala Tantra* (2.27.34.5), *dharana* is concentration on the six subtle centers of the chakras and the coiled power of Kundalini. Concentration on the chakras should be performed sequentially, starting from the first, the Muladhara Chakra, and gradually approaching the Sahasrara, the seventh chakra, which is the seat of supreme consciousness in individual consciousness. This practice creates habitual one-pointedness of the mind. By concentrating on the chakras one by one, and on Kundalini moving upward from the first to the seventh chakra, each chakra becomes a point for fixing the mind. When this concentration is accompanied by the special sounds *(mantras)* associated with each chakra, it elevates consciousness from the sensory level and brings forth a state of deep concentration, stilling the mental modifications *(vritties).*

The first step in *dharana* requires an *asana* that enhances concentration, a motionless body, and a calm mind. Then comes *pranayama.* When *dharana* becomes solid and firm, the suspension of breath *(kumbhaka)* is automatically prolonged, or else inhalation and exhalation are carried out unconsciously and the breath rate decreases, reducing the neuro-motor activity and the activity of the mind. After one can perform *pranayama* without any difficulty and can suspend breath effortlessly, the aspirant should concentrate on the mental repetition of the seed sounds *(bija mantras)* of the chakras during the *puraka, rechaka,* and *kumb-*

haka stages of *pranayama*. The seed sounds should be chanted internally, not with the vocal cords. The mind should be diverted to continuous mental production of these sounds. The processes of *puraka, rechaka,* and *kumbhaka* should not be able to interrupt this mental repetition of the mantras. Maintaining concentration on the seed sounds without being interrupted by respiration is *dharana.* However, fixing of the mind or maintaining concentration *(dharana)* is not the final goal; it is only a means of achieving the deep, unbroken, uninterrupted meditation of *dhyana.*

Each of the eight limbs of Ashtanga Yoga build upon each other. *Yama* and *niyama* prepare the aspirant for *asana,* and *asana* creates the ground for *pranayama.* *Pranayama* leads to *pratyahara,* and *pratyahara* to *dharana,* which leads to *dhyana* and *samadhi.* Thus all the steps work in coordination. *Yama* and *niyama* awaken the spiritual nature and *pranayama* awakens the dormant coiled spiritual energy. None of these steps can be avoided, and when one step is practiced enough that it becomes habitual, the others become easily possible.

For aspirants of Kundalini Yoga, concentration on the *bija mantras* means concentration on the chakras, which actually is concentration on Kundalini. This is a process of withdrawing mental energy from the perceptive field and holding it in the spiritual field. The *sadhaka* withdraws the mind from the senses by concentration on vital points. There are eighteen vital points mentioned in the scriptures: (1) foot, (2) big toe, (3) ankle, (4) leg, (5) knee, (6) thigh, (7) anus, (8) genital, (9) navel, (10) heart, (11) neck, (12) larynx, (13) palate, (14) nostrils, (15) eyes, (16) space between the eyebrows, (17) forehead, and (18) head. Of these the four most important are: (1) navel, (2) heart, (3) space between the eyebrows *(trikuti),* and (4) head (Sahasrara). When it is involved with the senses, the mind creates duality, and when it is withdrawn from the senses, this duality ends. When all mental modifications *(vritties)* are dissolved, the consciousness that has been conditioned by them achieves its natural state of non-duality.

In Tantra *dharana* (concentration) is done not just on the subtle centers (chakras) and the spiritual energy of Kundalini, but also on the spiritual heart, the individual consciousness *(jiva),* the Self (in *trikuti*), and Sahasrara. Traditionally, the heart has been recognized as the principal region for the fixation of the mind, as it is the center or seat of individual consciousness *(jiva).* This heart, though, is not the anatomical heart; it is not a part of the external or outer world, as the senses are completely withdrawn in *dharana*. In Kundalini Yoga, the spiritual heart *(ananda kanda)* is considered to be in the middle of an eight-petaled lotus within the fourth chakra (see illustration of the Anahata Chakra). Concentration on it during withdrawal *(pratyahara)* leads to renunciation. This helps *dharana* and leads to *dhyana*, uninterrupted deep meditation.

7. Dhyana – Uninterrupted Meditation

Dhyana is meditation, in which neither the *dhyata* (the one who is meditated upon) nor the *dhyana* (the consciousness of meditation) exist. When the aspirant reaches *dhyana*, the I-consciousness, the divinity as supreme consciousness, and the consciousness of *dhyana* (meditation), all disappear. The I-consciousness, the mind, and the intellect dissolve in Kundalini, and Kundalini dissolves in the supreme consciousness. *Dhyana,* therefore, is the revelation of pure consciousness, which cannot be described in words or experienced by the senses, mind, or intellect. It is like a drop merging in the ocean, becoming the ocean itself. Pure consciousness is like the ocean, and individual or I-consciousness is the merging drop. Pure consciousness, the supreme truth, cannot be reached by the senses, cognitive faculties, austerity, or other devices. It can only be experienced in *dhyana*.

This state can only be achieved after the body becomes motionless, spiritual energy is made to move through *pranayama* (especially *kumbhaka*), and concentration *(dharana)* is practiced in conjunction with mantra repetition. In *dharana* one concentrates on the chakras, Kundalini, and the supreme truth, but when the state of *dhyana* (deep meditation) comes, the consciousness of the chakras vanishes. The mind becomes still and self-consciousness or I-consciousness is lost, visualization ceases, the feeling of the continuous flow of energy in the spine vanishes, and the inner dialogue stops. The experience of bliss begins. Consciousness enters the fourth state *(turiya),* beyond the three normal states of wakefulness, dreaming, and deep sleep.

Dhyana is of two types: *saguna,* with form (*sa* - with, *guna* - attribute), and *nirguna*, without form (*nir* - without, *guna* - attribute). In Tantra, meditation on the chakras and their deities is with form until Kundalini pierces the sixth chakra. Then it becomes meditation on the formless supreme truth *(nirguna dhyana)*. This is the final stage of *dhyana*, the concentration on the supreme truth having no shape, form, or name. Although meditating on the formless, nameless, supreme truth is the summum bonum of *dhyana,* it can only be achieved by prolonged practice of concentration on the deities with form. It is the journey of the I-consciousness from percept to concept. It is said that a percept without a concept is empty and a concept without a percept is blind. The process of transcending from form to the formless is like learning the initially abstract letters of the alphabet. One learns 'A' by associating it with a concrete thing such as an apple. Then, after one has learned the alphabet, the apple for 'A', ball for 'B', and cat for 'C' disappear. One can then make words and communicate by combining the letters of the alphabet into words, sentences, and paragraphs. Just as the alphabet is helpful in learning a language, the divinities of the chakras are helpful in spiritualization of the cognitive, conative, and affective aspects of consciousness. Then, just as the letters disappear, the divinities with form also vanish when the formless divinity is reached.

Through purity of knowledge one starts seeing unity in diversity and the I-consciousness is purified and spiritualized. In such a state, all existence is the supreme consciousness *(sarva khal idam brahman),* the consciousness enters a state when *dhyana* is transformed into *samadhi,* and the supreme consciousness is revealed.

The fruit of *dharana* is *dhyana;* the fruit of *dhyana* is *samadhi.*

8. *Samadhi* – Uninterrupted *Dhyana*

The word *samadhi* is formed from three components: *sam* (equal, balanced, complete), *a* (eternal), and *dhi* (*buddhi,* cognition or knowledge). When a state of complete equilibrium is achieved, that is *samadhi.* For individual consciousness, *samadhi* is the state in which the I-consciousness disappears and becomes pure consciousness, free from the awareness of itself, time, and space. This is also called self-realization. In this state, the world outside and the world inside both disappear; only *ananda* (supreme bliss) remains. Consciousness is infinite, but the mind *(manas),* intellect *(buddhi),* and egotism *(ahamkara)* make it appear finite. Through *samadhi,* the realization of the infinite nature of consciousness makes the yogi free from the imprisonment of *manas, buddhi,* and *ahamkara.*

The regular practice of Ashtanga Yoga removes the sheaths of ever-changing *maya* (illusory existence). The Annamayi Kosha (the sheath of matter) is removed in *asana,* the Pranamayi Kosha (the sheath of vital air) in *pranayama,* the Manomayi

Kosha (the sheath of mind) in *dharana,* and the Vijnanamayi Kosha (the sheath of knowledge) in *dhyana.* The Self, which remains in the never-changing truth of Anandamayi Kosha (the sheath of bliss), becomes the only existing reality, and the state of tranquillity and bliss prevails. The individual self becomes the supreme Self. It is said in the *Saubhagyalakshmi Upanishad:* "As salt thrown into water becomes the same as water (dissolves completely), so the state in which the I-consciousness dissolves in the supreme consciousness is called *samadhi.*" As the drop is surrounded by the ocean, so is the self surrounded by the supreme Self.

The supreme Self is the supreme truth. The state of *samadhi* brings illumination, knowledge. Though a person in that state, when seen from the outside, looks like a motionless rock, the yogi is full of knowledge (truth), pure consciousness (being), abiding in bliss *(ananda),* known as *sat-chit-ananda.* God is not a person, whereas a yogi is a person, but a yogi is a person whose body is pure and in which the metabolism becomes so slow that one breath lasts for a long time.

After a prolonged state of *samadhi,* when a yogi again becomes conscious in a worldly sense, he or she stays in a state called *sahaja samadhi.* There is no need to practice Ashtanga Yoga anymore. There is no need to close the eyes to be detached from the sense of sight, for it is no longer the world that is seen, but the spark of the Divine in all forms. Every word or sound is heard as a mantra; every breath becomes *japa,* and every action becomes worship. If life has to continue, it continues, but the attitude of the yogi toward the phenomenal world changes. It is no longer the illusion of *maya,* but *lila,* the divine play. The yogi becomes an embodiment of love and peace. The entire environment in which he or she dwells changes, influencing others also to become tranquil and loving. The yogi becomes a mirror in which everyone can see him- or herself. He or she is the best friend, philosopher, and guide.

Samadhi is of two kinds: *samprajnata* and *asamprajnata.* In *samprajnata samadhi* the yogi achieves a state of super-conscious concentration, in which the I-consciousness dissolves in divine or supreme consciousness. In *asamprajnata samadhi,* the divine, God-consciousness also is not there; it is only blissful illumination. This state is indescribable in words, a bliss beyond any worldly pleasure and divine knowledge that gives enlightenment. This is not only experiencing *sat-chit-ananda* but being *sat-chit-ananda.*

According to Kundalini Yoga, *samadhi* is the union of Kundalini Shakti (the female principle) with Shiva (the male principle). Through the yearning for union, the aspirant's dormant energy (Shakti) awakens, ascends through the Sushumna path, reaches the abode of her Lord (Shiva), and unites with him. This union is only possible after proper purification of the Nadis, the recitation of seed sounds *(bija mantras),* and visualization exercises. Yogic *mudras* are also a valuable part of Kundalini Yoga.

The Yogic Mudras

A *mudra* is a specific kind of muscular control process used to help concentration, willful withdrawal of the senses, meditation, and the arousal and moving of the Kundalini Shakti. *Mudras* can be called meditation practices and are done in combination with *asanas* (postures) and *bandhas* (locks). There are eight such *mudras,* but three are considered to be primary.

1. Shambhavi or Sambhavi Mudra

Shambhavi Mudra is internal gazing. This *mudra* is especially useful in sensory control. Although generally in Yoga this *mudra* is concentration on the Ajna Chakra, or on the point between the eyebrows, with the eyes drawn upward so that the top of the iris is not visible, in Kundalini Yoga, Shambhavi Mudra entails internal meditation on the chakras as subtle centers and not as organs or areas of the body. The *sadhaka* (aspirant) meditates on the diagrams of the chakras that have been discovered by tantric visionaries through their inner vision. These images include the divine energies present in each of the chakras: the presiding deity, the Shakti, the seed sounds, the carrier of the *bija mantra,* and the *yantra* (the diagram of the element in geometrical form).

To help prepare for meditation on the chakras, the *sadhaka* should first color the images of the chakras (given in chapter 3, "The Essentials of the Chakras") to establish them in the mind's eye. When one colors the images, they are retained in the mind and internal visualization becomes easy.

The meditation on and visualization of the chakras is done in gradual progression, beginning with the first chakra and continuing up through the second, third, and so on. The center of concentration should be the chakras and not the gross organs of the body. Yogic schools that provide no images of chakras can only suggest that the *sadhaka* should meditate on the heart or between the eyebrows. However, this keeps the focus on the body, whereas the goal in Kundalini Yoga is to go beyond body consciousness. In Kundalini meditation, one gets absorbed in the abstract *yantras,* mantras, and deities of the chakras, which spiritualizes the consciousness. Thus tantric visualization aided by coloring the images of the chakras is a much more efficacious practice.

When the mind and breath are absorbed in the internal image and the pupils of the eyes are motionless (even though the eyes are open they do not register external images), Shambhavi Mudra is achieved.

2. Khechari Mudra

Khechari Mudra (*khe - akasha, chari -* dwelling) is dwelling in the *akasha* (space), which is located between the Ida and Pingala Nadis, at the center of the eyebrows. When *prana* is directed to remain steady in the Sushumna in the supporting space between the eyebrows, Khechari Mudra is attained. The tongue should be turned upward to the roof of the palate; this *mudra* is also called "swallowing the tongue." In order to execute this *mudra,* the tongue should be made soft and elongated. This is done in two ways. One is to wrap the tongue with a soft, wet, fine cloth and "milk" it. The other is by performing the lingual exercise of alternately retracting and stretching the tongue. When the palate region is pressed with the tongue, *soma* (nectar), a cool, life-giving substance, flows down from the Soma Chakra. This restores the body, making it free from diseases, so the life of the yogi is prolonged. The yogi gains control over hunger and thirst. By practicing Khechari Mudra the *sadhaka* also attains mastery over the fluctuations of the mind and achieves *turiya,* the state of unconscious consciousness. The *sadhaka* should practice Khechari Mudra until *yoga nidra* (yoga sleep) is experienced.

When the external breath is stopped by performing this *mudra*—for swallowing the tongue blocks the passage of air between the nostrils and the lungs— the breath within the body is suspended. *Prana,* along with the mind, becomes still within the Brahma Randhra, the void between the hemispheres of the brain. Concentration on Kundalini in this state brings about the final fusion of Kundalini, *prana,* and the mind. The union between Shiva and Shakti takes place and the highest goal of the true aspirant is thus achieved.

3. Yoni Mudra

Yoni Mudra is anogenital control. This *mudra* is very important because it helps to prevent the downward flow of *apana.* The whole process of rousing Kundalini is the control of *apana (vayu* that operates in the region below the navel). Yoni Mudra helps the withdrawal of *apana vayu* from the body and especially from the area of the lower abdominal tract where its concentration is greatest. *Apana* becomes concentrated in the Svadhishthana Chakra (the second chakra) as *kandarpa* (sexual) energy. When it is released, it becomes a strong desire for the enjoyment of sexual pleasure. Through Yoni Mudra *apana* is withdrawn; then the *kandarpa* energy can be directed upward with the help of internal *mantra japa,* repetition of the seed sounds of the Muladhara Chakra and the Svadhishthana Chakra. Then the practice of the adamantine control exercise *(vajrauli)* becomes possible. Yoni Mudra thus is the first step towards the practice of *vajrauli,* the upward movement of sexual energy.

The Yoni Mudra is performed by assuming the "accomplished" posture *(siddhasana)* with pressure put on the perineum by the left heel and pressure put on the hypogastric region of the abdomen (the median region of the abdominal wall) by the right heel. First one concentrates on the Muladhara Chakra. Then the aspirant should either breathe through both the nostrils or through the mouth by making the lips resemble the beak of a crow. While inhaling one should contract the anus and genitals forcefully and do abdominal retraction. Then the aspirant should use the Jalandhara Bandha (chin lock) while continuing to contract the anogenital muscles, performing Uddiyana Bandha (abdominal lock), while the breath is suspended *(kumbhaka).* Holding of the breath should be done as long as possible without too much strain. Then the breath should be exhaled slowly and the *sadhaka* should relax the neck and abdominal muscles. After relaxing, the *sadhaka* should repeat the same process. All the while, Kundalini Shakti in her luminous form should be meditated upon.

These techniques all aid in the process of arousing the spiritual energy of Kundalini and the upward movement of that energy in the Sushumna path.

However, there are obstructions in the path that are known as knots *(granthis)*. Untying these knots frees the yogi from the physical body, the astral body, and the causal body.

The Knots *(Granthis)*

The word *granthi* literally means "a knot." There are three main knots in the Sushumna that represent the three aspects of consciousness: knowing, feeling, and doing. The Brahma Granthi (the knot of Brahma) is feeling and the mind; the Vishnu Granthi (the knot of Vishnu) is doing and *prana;* and Rudra Granthi (the knot of Rudra) is knowing and *jnana* (true knowledge). When the three

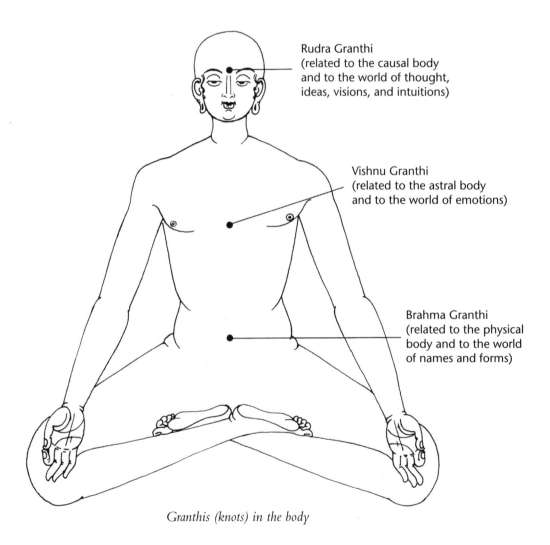

Rudra Granthi
(related to the causal body
and to the world of thought,
ideas, visions, and intuitions)

Vishnu Granthi
(related to the astral body
and to the world of emotions)

Brahma Granthi
(related to the physical
body and to the world
of names and forms)

Granthis (knots) in the body

knots are untied, phenomenal reality becomes pervaded by divine energy and the self becomes established in the Sheath of Bliss (Anandamayi Kosha).

Brahma Granthi

Brahma Granthi is the first knot. The *Jabal Upanishad* and the *Yogashikha Upanishad* state that this *granthi* is located in the Muladhara Chakra, the first chakra, because Brahma is the presiding deity of Muladhara. However, most tantric scriptures place it in the Manipura Chakra, the third chakra, because it is the location of the fire element, which is linked to the principle of form *(rupa)*. Brahma Granthi is the knot of the phenomenal world *(samsara)*, the world of names and forms *(nama-rupa)*, the first obstacle in the growth of the spiritual aspect of the individual self *(jiva)*.

The world is created by Brahma, but the world known to the individual consciousness is created by the mind. Through its attachments the mind creates meanings in the illusory world, and the relationship between the individual self and *samsara* is created. Thus, for the individual, the world created by Brahma is real as long as the mind works. Shankaracharya, in his *Viveka Chudamani,* clearly says that the mind is *maya* (ever-changing illusory existence). In deep sleep, when the mind does not work, the phenomenal world disappears. In the dream state, when the mind starts functioning again, the world is re-created by the mind. The world created by the mind is as true to the dreaming self as the world perceived by the *jiva* in the waking state, but both are unreal *(maya)*. When one is detached, this relationship between the mind and the phenomenal world disappears.

As long as the attributes of the phenomenal world and its relationships make sense, the Kundalini energy cannot dissolve in the supreme truth. It keeps on rotating in the lower chakras and occupies a great deal of the aspirant's consciousness. Desires and ambitions trap the mental energy. Untying this knot frees one from the bondage caused by attachment. Until one unties this knot, one cannot meditate effectively because it creates restlessness and prevents the mind from becoming one-pointed *(ekagra)*.

To be detached from the phenomenal world one has to live a disciplined life. When the body chemistry is purified by the practice of the *Kshata Karmas (dhauti, vasti, neti, trataka, nauli,* and *kapalabhati)* and the use of *mudras,* the dormant spiritual nature becomes active. But living a disciplined life also means following the steps of Ashtanga Yoga *(yama, niyama, asana, pranayama, pratyahara, dharana, dhyana,* and *samprajnata samadhi),* without which union with supreme truth *(asamprajnata samadhi)* is not possible.

Even after having done all these steps, one cannot achieve the highest state without a suitable natural environment and the presence of a kind, loving, and experienced guru. The guru should be one who has been properly initiated in the path of Kundalini Yoga. His or her presence will produce calmness and make the mind still. Faith in the guru and the grace of the Kundalini Shakti can produce miraculous effects, and the knot can be untied. The aspirant becomes centered and calm, and images from the world of names and forms do not interrupt the meditation. Diversity becomes unity and all objects become divine.

Vishnu Granthi

Vishnu Granthi is located in the area of Anahata Chakra (the heart center), which is also the seat of *prana.* Vishnu is the preserver and, as the vital life force, *prana* is the preserver of life in the organism. *Prana* controls the mind and the emotions. The Heart Chakra is the seat of devotion, faith, love, and compassion. Vishnu is the lord of compassion, because preservation needs compassion. Compassion presents obstacles in the path of Kundalini because it creates attachment, diverting energy toward the world outside. It is not attachment to the desires of the mind, nor to the objects that gratify the senses, but attachment to the cosmic good and a keen desire to help suffering humanity. This attachment makes one a dreamer, a reformer, a savior, a preserver of ancient knowledge—a person of high spiritual qualities—but not a yogi. The aspirant is still tied to the world, and connected with spiritual orders and organizations that help humanity at large. Instead of going back to the source through union, one adopts a *bodhisattva* vow to relieve the world from suffering and willfully gets caught by the cycle of life and death.

The aspirant has to untie this knot, which creates emotional ties to traditions and idealism, thus trapping the energy at the Heart Chakra. By true discrimination, one has to realize the purpose behind the cosmos, the divine plan, and liberate oneself from the attachment to doing, to preservation. The world is illusion; thus the suffering and pain of that world cannot be real. A compassionate person is conscious of the unity in diversity, but because of this knot, remains caught by diversity. Although the mind of such a person is under control, centered, one-pointed *(ekagra)*, it becomes restless *(vyagra)* and does not achieve the *niruddha* state, in which it is devoid of thoughts.

Vishnu Granthi is difficult to untie, because of its placement in the Heart Chakra, its balanced state between materialism and idealism, and its connection with the genetic code. To untie this knot one has to do *pranayama,* in which all thoughts and ideas are eliminated and the aspirant becomes unconcerned with worldly pleasure and pain. There is no liking or disliking; the consciousness is free from waves and is absolutely tranquil. Through yogic *sadhana* of *prana* one can even achieve freedom from the deep-rooted bondage of the genetic code. Freedom from all bondage is the goal of life, but this freedom will not be complete until the aspirant is released from I-consciousness, which happens with the untying of the final knot.

Rudra Granthi

Rudra Granthi is located in the area of the Ajna Chakra, the area of the third eye. Rudra is the destroyer and so is true knowledge *(jnana)*. There is nothing to destroy except the illusion that is I-consciousness or ego. With the untying of the Brahma Granthi, the illusory world of names and forms is annihilated, and with the untying of the Vishnu Granthi, the attachment to the fruits of actions ends. Finally, one must get beyond the attachment to I-consciousness, which obstructs the path of Kundalini on its way to Soma Chakra where the supreme truth is realized and non-dual consciousness is achieved. The I-consciousness is like "drop-consciousness" and the truth is the ocean of pure consciousness. The drop and the ocean are one, but the I-consciousness of the drop keeps it separated. As long as this consciousness remains, one goes through the cycle of life and death. It makes the infinite finite and time-bound. This illusion must be destroyed.

When Kundalini reaches the Ajna Chakra, the aspirant, who is now a yogi, transcends the phenomenal world. The tantric scriptures state that a yogi who reaches Ajna Chakra achieves *siddhis* such as: the power to see what is happening anywhere at any time—past, present, and future; the power to be present in any place at any time or many places at the same time; and the power to disappear and reappear. The elements in their gross form no longer bind the yogi in a particular form. The process of aging stops. Mind and *prana* are no longer obstacles, but at this point, the Rudra Granthi can become an obstacle if I-consciousness remains. One can become attached to the *siddhis* (the powers that create miracles). But if the yogi has no I-consciousness, there is no "I" to get attached. Thus, the I-consciousness has to be destroyed.

The aspirant who has reached the Ajna Chakra has gone beyond the elements that continuously change the make-up of the physical body and cause emotional fluctuations and attachments in the individual consciousness. Thus, in the Ajna Chakra, the yogi is able to establish himself or herself in infinity and then Rudra Granthi unties itself. The passage to the Sushumna clears and Kundalini reaches Soma Chakra. The yogi transcends the three *gunas (sattva, rajas,* and *tamas)* to become *gunatit* (beyond the three *gunas)* and the consciousness is established in eternal bliss, complete union through non-dual consciousness.

The Ten Sounds

During the process of working through the knots the yogi listens to ten kinds of sounds that help in achieving a state of deep meditation:

1. The chirping of birds
2. The sound of crickets
3. The sound of bells
4. The sound of the conch
5. The sound of the *vina* (Indian lute)
6. The sound of the *mridanga* (barrel drum)
7. The sound of the flute
8. The sound of the *pakhavaj* (another type of drum)
9. The sound of the trumpet
10. The roar of a lion

Movements of Kundalini

When the Kundalini energy rises, all the mental *(manovahi)* Nadis become active. When the combustion of *prana* and *apana* takes place and Kundalini Shakti moves upward with great force through the Brahma Nadi, piercing all the chakras, she can move in different styles, depending upon which element is dominant in the person:

- Ant-like movement: When the earth element *(prithvi)* is dominant, a creeping sensation is felt at the base of the spine.

- Frog-like movement: When the water element *(apah)* is dominant, a throbbing sensation is felt in the spine: now strong, now weak. It also feels like hopping and stopping, and hopping again.

- Serpent-like movement: When the fire element *(agni)* is dominant, a feeling of excessive heat or of fire is felt in the area of the navel and the sensation of the rising of a fiery stream in the spine is experienced. It is under the influence of the fire element that Kundalini is sometimes experienced as terrifying fiery energy.

- Bird-like movement: When the air element *(vayu)* is dominant, a feeling of levitation, lightness, weightlessness, or the feeling of a sweeping, floating movement is felt in the spine. The movement is regular and the feeling is often in the region of the heart. A vision of light may be experienced in the heart region, or a cold sensation in the spine may be felt.

- Monkey-like movement: When *akasha* (space/ether) is dominant, a feeling of jumping is experienced. In this state Kundalini moves with such force that many chakras are crossed in one leap. In *akasha* the movement is not as steady as in the earth element, not as fluid as in the water element, and not as fiery as in the fire element. It comes like a storm and ascends to the highest center in no time.

By regular practice of the eight steps of Ashtanga Yoga, the aspirant will acquire a spiritual attitude. *Asanas* bring an end to all corporeal activities, and actions are confined to *prana* and the sense organs. Through the suspension of breath arrived at by *pranayama,* the movement of *prana* and the sense organs ceases; only mental activity remains. By *pratyahara, dharana, dhyana,* and *samprajnata samadhi,* mental activity ceases and action exists in the *buddhi,* or the higher mind, alone. By letting go of all attachments and by long and regular practice of *samprajnata,* the yogi achieves a natural state of being that is an unchangeable state, the final aim of Yoga. The yogi then stays forever in union with supreme consciousness *(asamprajnata samadhi),* in a state of blissful illumination.

The elements of the chakras

The Essentials of the Chakras

In the *Shiva Samhita* (ch. 2), Shiva clearly states the well-known yogic statement, "As it is in the macrocosm, so it is in the microcosm." He says:

Dehe asmin vartte meru sapt deep samanvita,
Sarita sagar shaila kshetrani kshetrapalika.
Rishyo munaye sarve nakshatrani grahastatha,
Punya teerthani peethani vartante peeth devata.
Srishti samhar kartarau bhramante shashi bhaskaro,
Nabho vayusch vannhishcha jalam prithvi tathaivcha.
Trailokye yani bhutani tani sarvani dehta,
Meru sam veshtya sarvatra vyavhara pravartate.
Janati ya sarvamidam sa yogi natra samshaya,
Brahmand sangyake dehe yatha desham vyavisthita.

An aspirant of Yoga should see in his own spine *(meru)* the seven islands (chakras), the rivers, the oceans, the mountains, the guardians of the eight directions, the seers *(rishis),* the sages *(munis),* the stars and planets and all the constellations, all holy places *(tirthas),* the special power places *(siddha peethas)* and their divinities, the sun and moon, and the prime source of creation, preservation, and destruction. He should see in the microcosm of his own body the five basic elements *(akasha,* air, fire, water, and earth) and whatever else exists in the three worlds *(lokas)* of the macrocosm. All these are supported by the spine *(meru)* and exist in the spine. One who knows this secret is in fact a yogi, there is no doubt about it.

71

This makes it clear that chakras are subtle centers located in the spinal cord and not in the gross nervous plexuses, which are outside of the vertebral column. At the same time, the chakras are the playground of the elements, the building blocks of all psychophysical existence. The five elements arise from the five *tanmatras:* sound *(shabda)*, smell *(gandha)*, taste *(rasa)*, form *(rupa)*, and touch *(sparsha)*. Tanmatra literally means "only that" *(tan* - that, *matra* - only). *Tanmatras* are pure frequencies or essences. It has been said: "Sound creates void *(akasha)*, as smell creates earth, taste creates water; form creates fire, and touch creates air" *(shabda*

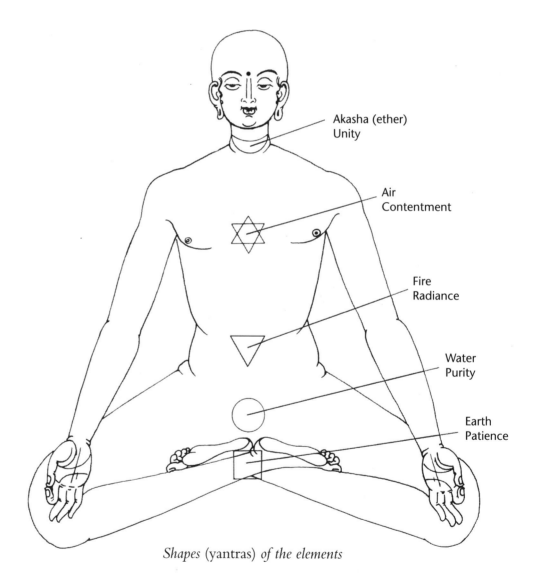

Shapes (yantras) *of the elements*

Akasha (ether)
Unity

Air
Contentment

Fire
Radiance

Water
Purity

Earth
Patience

gunakam *akasham shabda).* From the *tanmatras* evolve the elements *(mahabhutas)* and from the *mahabhutas* evolve the sense organs and work organs *(indriyas).* Although the chakras are subtle, they have a definite relationship with the gross material field of the body and its functions. Each of the first five chakras is associated with a specific element: the Muladhara Chakra with earth, the Svadhishthana Chakra with water, the Manipura Chakra with fire, the Anahata Chakra with air, and the Vishuddha Chakra with *akasha.* The *tanmatras* are each related with a sense principle, so each chakra is also connected with a specific sense organ.

In a living body the material and non-material fields are interpenetrating. Breathing is a neuro-motor activity that activates all the systems that exist in the body. It brings in *prana,* the vital life force, which works with both the material and non-material aspects of the individual organism. Svara Yoga (the yoga of nasal breath) clearly shows that the chakras are the playground of the subtle *tanmatra-mahabhuta* forces. In the 900 breaths taken every hour, there is a cycle of nasal breathing in which each of the elements dominates for a period of time. Each chakra is vitalized when energy flows in the element with which that chakra is connected. During each cycle of nasal breathing through one nostril—right or left—the air element (influencing the fourth chakra) dominates for eight minutes, then the fire element (third chakra) for twelve minutes, then the earth element (first chakra) for twenty minutes, then the water element (second chakra) for sixteen minutes, then *akasha* (fifth chakra) for four minutes. Along with the normal operation of the chakras determined by this oscillating breathing, all of the Nadis, except the Sushumna, are active. Within the last minute—for a brief period of 10 breaths—both nostrils work together, activating the otherwise dormant Sushumna Nadi. Then the whole cycle starts over again in the other nostril.

However, it is important to understand that this working of the chakras, and the brief activation of the Sushumna, is very different from the piercing of the chakras by the aroused energy of Kundalini moving upward in the Sushumna Nadi. The chakras are psychic centers as well as centers of transformation of psychic or mental energy into spiritual energy. Each chakra is a storehouse of various kinds of psychophysical energies that are activated by the breath when the energy passes from one chakra to the other with the flow of the elements. *Prana* enters the body through the nasal breath and works on both the gross material level as well as on the subtle level. The subtle energies are forces of the *tanmatra-mahabhuta* combination. Each *tanmatra* force is represented by a seed sound *(bija mantra)* composed of sound frequencies *(dhvani)*, sound power *(sphota)*, and a *bindu*, which is the conscious form. The sound frequencies and their inherent powers are expressed as deities. The power of the *bindu*, which is consciousness, controls all the forces operating in a chakra.

The descriptions of each chakra in the sections to follow include the psychophysical and *tanmatra-mahabhuta* energies that operate in each chakra:

- ∞ Element, including its Shape *(Yantra)* and Color
- ∞ Predominant Sense
- ∞ Aspects
- ∞ Seed Sound *(Bija Mantra),* including its Carrier *(Vahana)* and Color
- ∞ Presiding Deity
- ∞ Shakti (Form of Kundalini)
- ∞ Sense Organ
- ∞ Work Organ
- ∞ Air *(Vayu, Prana)*
- ∞ Plane *(Loka)*
- ∞ Ruling Planet

According to the *Rudrayamala Tantra* the chakras are within the innermost core of the Sushumna Nadi, known as the Brahma Nadi, which is the carrier of spiritual energy. (For more detail about the Nadis, see pages 29–42 in chapter 2, "Kundalini and Yoga.") When the coiled spiritual energy (Kundalini) is aroused by the practices of Yoga, the dormant Kundalini leaves its abode in the Muladhara Chakra and moves upward in the Brahma Nadi within the Sushumna Nadi. The pranic force is withdrawn from all the other Nadis and concentrated in the Sushumna, which causes the suspension of breath. At that time, the normal function of the chakras as psychic centers ceases and they begin to function as centers of transformation of psychophysical energy into spiritual energy. When the spiritual energy becomes operative, Kundalini absorbs all the

Muladhara Chakra

Svadhishthana Chakra

Manipura Chakra

Anahata Chakra

Vishuddha Chakra

Ajna Chakra

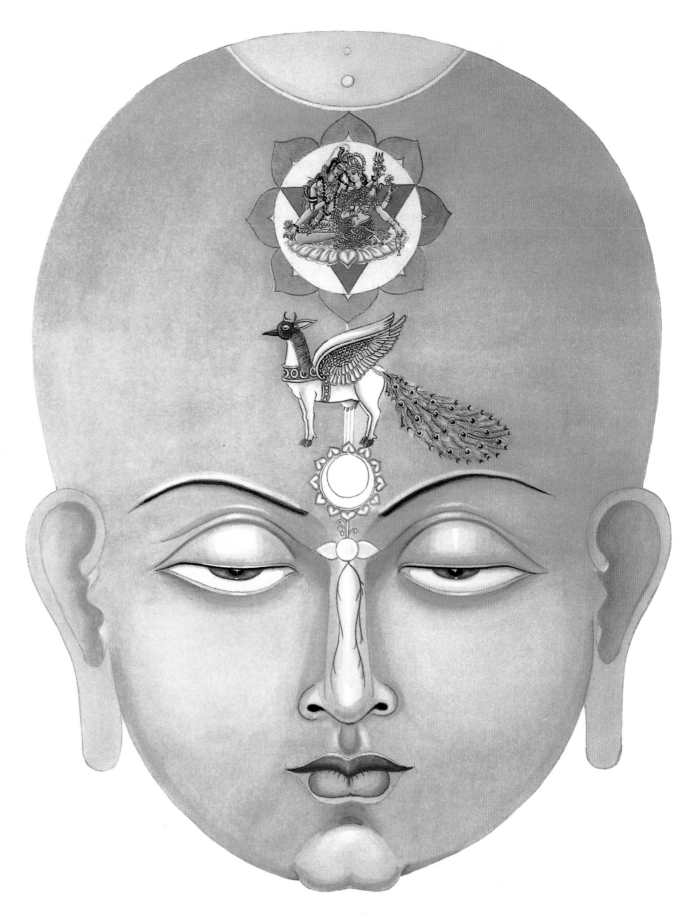

Soma Chakra

Sahasrara Chakra

other energies of the chakras—of the elements, mantras, the sense and work organs, *prana,* the presiding deities and Shaktis—and moves upward through Brahma Nadi. When the roused Kundalini passes through the different chakras, various spiritual experiences occur. The normal function of the chakras is restored with everything as it was when Kundalini comes back to Muladhara and coils up again.

Chakra meditation is a great help to yoga aspirants as well as to people who are living in the world (have not renounced the world). When an aspirant works on the chakras, the task is to make the chakra inactive by arousing the upward flow of Kundalini energy through the chakra. The influence of the five elements on the first five chakras is depicted in the illustration of each chakra by the particular shape *(yantra)* of that element. Traditionally, each chakra is seen in the form of a lotus—a circle around the *yantra,* surrounded by a particular number of petals. The petals are the seats of mental modifications *(vritties)* and connected desires. Mental modifications are a mode of our being and are maintained by sense functioning. All of the *vritties* do not work all the time but some *vritti* is always occupying the mind. It is said that the lotus petals are normally pointing downward, causing energy to flow down, but when the Kundalini Shakti rises, the petals go up like a blossoming lotus. This upward movement of the petals blocks the downward flow of energy and acts like a lock.

In the chakras, each petal has a seed sound *(bija mantra)* associated with it. The *bija mantras* are sound frequencies used to invoke the divine energy inside the body. The seed sound is the storehouse of divinity in a most concentrated form. This latent power of the deity is aroused by producing the sound in an appropriate manner. The process of producing sound in the right way can only be learned directly from a guru. When the disciple learns to produce the sound correctly, it quickly produces the desired effect of invoking divine energy. The sound aspect of the mantra assumes the form of the divinity connected with the mantra and leads the disciple to the state of deep uninterrupted concentration. When the divinities are invoked by seed sounds, they are absorbed in the Kundalini as the uncoiled energy moves upward. The chakras stop working when Kundalini rises and breath is suspended. When breathing begins again,

Sounds of the Chakras

the chakras are reactivated and the game of *prana*, the mind, ego, and intellect resumes.

In the worldly way, we try to refine the behavior of the individual unit of consciousness by adopting control devices and harmonizing the influence of the chakras. Energy flows through the chakras and is transformed by them. Behavior is influenced by the elements, pranic energy, the mind, intellect, and ego. Although the energy changes with the element, the obsessions of the mind and ego compel the intellect to constantly think about the desires that occupy the mind. Thus, the mind creates the individual's world. Ego decides what is important and what is not. Intellect finds out the ways to act and methods to achieve the desired goal. In this way the world is not the world outside, but the world with which one mentally associates.

Chakras can be thought of as wheels of the mind that dwell in the forest of desires. And desires, like wheels themselves, are great motivating forces. Each chakra is a stage by stage playground of desires, exhibiting its influence on the persons who are attached to the enjoyment of that particular chakra. Throughout life, one dwells in this forest and thinks and understands life's situations from the standpoint of the chakras in which one normally feels most comfortable. Each chakra becomes a stage for the psychodrama of electrochemical energy that expresses itself as behavior in human beings. As a result, there are specific behavioral characteristics associated with each of the chakras.

As tools of the elements, the first five chakras create internal environments that change in accordance with the energy of the element being radiated. These changes lead to changes in desires and moods that can cause the same person to behave differently at different times. For example, as a result of the influence of the five elements, the concept of security is different for each of the first five chakras: in the first chakra security is job and shelter; in the second chakra it is personal beauty and youth; in the third chakra it is authority and status; in the fourth chakra it is faith; in the fifth chakra it is knowledge.

Chakras are important to yogis as transformers of mental energy into spiritual energy; they can be equally interesting to psychologists because of their influence on the play of mental energy, which creates moments of joy and disgust. Desires create pleasure and pain and those who have no endurance to bear pain become sick. Knowledge of chakras can help these weak people by giving them the assurance of change and improvement, putting a mirror in front of their faces to show them their behavioral pattern and helping them to confront themselves. Meditating on the appropriate chakra can do a great job in helping a person overcome mental modifications and emotional fluctuations. Psychotherapists and psychologists can make use of the energy transformation made possible by chakra meditation,

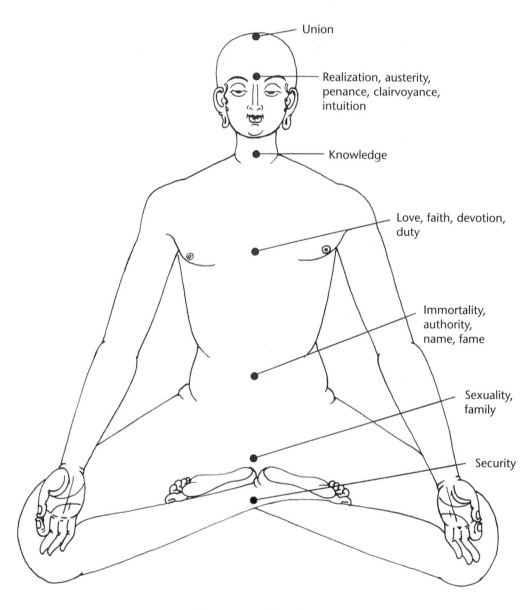

Union

Realization, austerity,
penance, clairvoyance,
intuition

Knowledge

Love, faith, devotion,
duty

Immortality,
authority,
name, fame

Sexuality,
family

Security

Desires and obstacles

but in order to know which chakra meditation would help a particular patient, they need to know the behavioral characteristics of the chakras. Thus, the descriptions of the chakras that follow also include the behavioral characteristics associated with each chakra. These are usually not found in Yoga books, because the final result of Yoga practices frees a person from all influence of the chakras.

The meditation on the chakras taught by Tantra Yoga involves all aspects of the Ashtanga Yoga given in detail in chapter 2, "Kundalini and Yoga." After following the *yamas* and *niyamas,* assuming a stable posture *(asana),* and mastering breath control *(pranayama),* the aspirant becomes an adept in the path of Yoga. Then comes withdrawal from the senses *(pratyahara)* and concentration *(dharana).* All of these steps are necessary to achieve the power to meditate *(dhyana),* which is real Yoga. The first step in meditation is the purification of the five elements *(tattvas),* their source *(the five tanmatras),* and the *indriyas* (the five sense organs and the five work organs). This process of purification, known as *bhuta shuddhi,* is effected by their absorption in Kundalini Shakti. Rousing of Kundalini therefore is the primary concern of an aspirant.

In *bhuta shuddhi* (purification of the elements), earth dissolves in water, water evaporates in fire, fire merges into air, and air disperses into *akasha* (the void). All of the principles associated with the earth element present in the first chakra are absorbed into the water element. Then the water element (and all the principles associated with it) are absorbed into the fire element, and so on. The elements *(tattvas* or *bhutas)* are not pure like the *tanmatras;* they are mixtures. The element earth is a combination of all five *bhutas: akasha,* air, fire, water, and earth. Water is a mixture of *akasha,* air, fire, and water; fire is a mixture of *akasha,* air, and fire; air is a mixture of *akasha* and air. *Akasha* is in essence having all yet being nothing (void). That is why *akasha* is the purest and lightest. Air is heavier than *akasha,* fire is heavier than air, water is heavier than fire, and earth is the heaviest and densest of all. The process of absorption of the elements and their principles is accomplished when *pranayama,* particularly the suspension of breath *(kumbhaka),* is done in conjunction with repetition of the seed sounds that are present in each chakra as the *bija mantras* of the elements and the lotus petals. Performing *pranayama* along with the repetition of AUM, or concentrating on the Ajna Chakra along

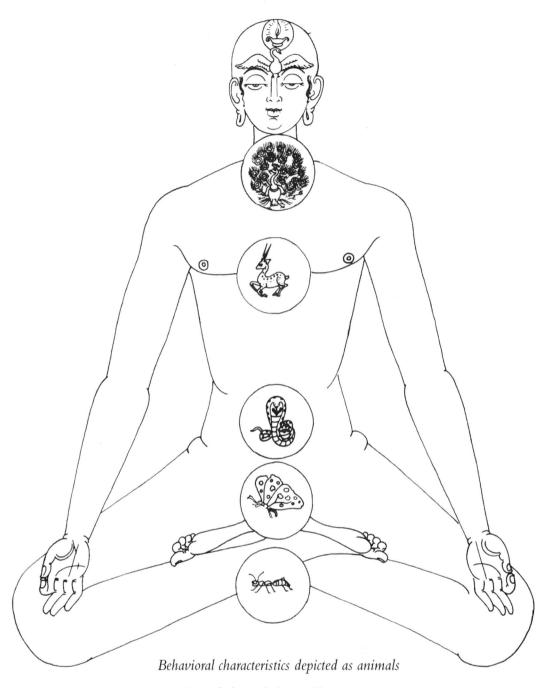

Behavioral characteristics depicted as animals

First chakra – behaves like an ant

Second chakra – behaves like a butterfly

Third chakra – behaves like a cobra

Fourth chakra – behaves like a deer running after a mirage

Fifth chakra – behaves like a peacock

Sixth chakra – behaves like a swan *(hamsa)*

Seventh chakra – pure illumination

with repetition of the mantra SOHAM are two examples of methods used to purify the elements and the mind. *Bhuta shuddhi* is automatically accomplished by following the path of devotion *(bhakti)*.

In whatever way it is accomplished, *bhuta shuddhi* is necessary for the arousal of Kundalini. Only after all of the elements and their associated principles are absorbed into *akasha* can the Kundalini energy be directed towards the Ajna Chakra where the I-consciousness is absorbed into super-consciousness *(samprajnata samadhi)*. Ultimately, Kundalini is absorbed in the Param Shiva, the supreme consciousness, the source of all spiritual consciousness *(asamprajnata samadhi)*. After the flow of Kundalini energy has reached the higher centers, the total attitude of the practitioner changes. This change is referred to repeatedly as a new birth and the aspirant is called "twice born." Maintaining the upward flow of energy then becomes the primary concern of the aspirant.

The constant, simultaneous practice of visualization and repetition of the seed sounds *(mantra japa)* helps the aspirant to maintain the flow of energy in the higher centers and thus get beyond the influence of the elements. Meditation on the chakras should be done using the image of the chakra that includes the respective element and divinities, not on a particular physical point such as the coccyx, base of the spine, or anal region. The physical areas associated with the chakras are only the locations of the related sense organs and work organs. The chakras themselves are related to the source of energy that puts life in the cellular body *(prana* and the elements). Thus, for example, the desires of the first chakra are not the desires of the anal region.

We must remember that energy flows through the chakras before it reaches the sense mind where it gets converted into the form of a dialogue or desire. Each breath works with one of the elements and the related chakra. All of the chakras do not work together; they work according to their related element. Meditation done without the related element will require more energy because it will not be aided by the element, but this meditation will still influence the breathing pattern and calm the mind.

Meditation on the Muladhara Chakra in the presence of the element earth develops natural health, strength of the body, and intellectual power. It prolongs life.

Meditation on the Svadhishthana Chakra in the presence of the element water frees the body from disease, gives one more vitality, sensitivity, intellectual power, and artistic ability, and makes one attractive to the opposite sex.

Meditation on the Manipura Chakra in the presence of the element fire develops natural immunity of the body, leads to the attainment of a long life, and releases certain uncommon powers of command, authority, organization, leadership, and management.

Meditation on the Anahata Chakra in the presence of the element air develops inner beauty and personal magnetism (ojas), making the body highly attractive (not only to the opposite sex). It develops the power of the intellect and leads to intellectual development above the normal standard. It enables the acquisition of uncommon sensory powers (ESP), poetic powers, and writing abilities.

Meditation on the Vishuddha Chakra in the presence of the element akasha generates adamantine hardness and strength, the power of absorption in deep meditation, the revelation of knowledge beyond written words, and the power to explain and clarify.

Meditation on the Ajna Chakra in the presence of the Sushumna gives non-dual consciousness and healing powers. It develops intuition and the power to see past, present, and future.

Meditation on the chakras starts with assuming a comfortable posture (asana), sitting on a seat made of some organic material (preferably not cotton), with the hands in the lap and the palms facing upwards. One should do five breath control exercises (pranayama) before commencing visualization. There should be a little pause between pranayama and visualization. Visualization should be practiced only when one's breathing does not interrupt one's concentration.

Visualization requires proper images of the chakras. The images of the chakras drawn by visionary artists of the past should be used. The illustrations in this book represent all the major components of each chakra and will help the mind to visualize and retain the images of the chakras. Coloring the line drawings in a systematic way can further help in visualization, for one can repeat in the mind the sequence in which the colors are painted. To achieve the proper colors, one should consult the color illustrations that are provided (see pages 74A–74H).

The following order should be used in coloring the chakras:

- The petals of the chakra
- The *yantra* of the chakra
- The animal that carries the seed sound *(bija mantra)*
- The seed sound
- The Shakti of the chakra
- The deity of the chakra

The same order should be used in visualization. By mentally reconstructing the complete drawing of the chakra, one can develop the practice of abstract visualization, which in time will lead to deep meditation.

However, such a tool without precepts is meaningless. Similarly, precepts without the proper tools offer no real growth. The line drawings should be colored to activate the right hemisphere of the brain; the text should be studied to enrich the understanding and activate the left hemisphere. This will create a balance between the "thinker's brain" and the "artist's brain." This will change the pattern of the brain waves and the psychic makeup. Repetition of the seed sounds and following the law of *dharma* (righteousness, order) will assist the aspirant in achieving higher states of consciousness.

Muladhara Chakra

मूलाधार चक्र

Bija petal sound

वं शं षं सं

MULADHARA CHAKRA
(FIRST CHAKRA)

Names:	Muladhara, Adhara
Meanings of the Names:	Foundation, Base (*mul* - base, *adhara* - support)
Location:	Perineum, below the genitals and above the anus inside the coccyx, the pelvic plexus, base of the spine, the first three vertebrae
Element *(Tattva):*	Earth
Color of the Element:	Yellow
Shape *(Yantra)* of the Element:	Square
Seed Sound *(Bija Mantra)* of the Element:	*LANG*
Color of the Seed Sound:	Gold
Carrier *(Vahana)* of the Seed Sound:	The elephant Airavata
Number of Petals:	Four
Color of the Petals:	Vermilion, blood red
Seed Sounds of the Petals:	*VANG, SHANG, KSHANG, SANG*
Aspects:	Security
Predominant Sense:	Smell
Sense Organ:	Nose
Work Organ:	Anus
Air *(Vayu, Prana):*	*Apana:* the air that expels the semen from the male organ and urine from sexes, and that which pushes the both child from the womb during birth
Plane *(Loka):*	Physical plane *(Bhu Loka)*
Ruling Planet:	Mars (solar, masculine)

Yantra **Form:** Square of chrome yellow color. The square is a symbol for earth. It has great significance with regard to earthly awareness, as it represents the earth itself, the four dimensions, and the four directions. The four points form the four pillars or corners of what is known as the quadrangular earth. This *yantra* is the seat of the seed sound *(bija mantra) LANG* and releases sound in all of the eight directions. This is often depicted by eight spears emanating from the square. All the divinities, the important Nadis (Ida, Pingala, Sushumna), the Svayambhu Lingam, and Goddess Kundalini reside inside the triangle which is the center of this *yantra.*

The Circle with Four Petals: The square is surrounded by a circle and four lotus petals. The four petals represent the four important mental modifications *(vritties):* (1) state of greatest joy *(paramananda);* (2) state of natural pleasure *(sahajananda);* (3) the delight in the control of passions *(virananda);* (4) the blissfulness in concentration *(yogananda),* as stated in *Mahanirvana Tantra.* The color of the petals is vermilion, a red with a yellowish tinge. It is mixed with a small touch of crimson red which gives the petals the color of blood *(shonita).*

The Triangle: The downward-pointing triangle in the pericarp is very important because it is the seat of the dormant vital life force, Kundalini Shakti, depicted in the form of a serpent coiled around the Svayambhu Lingam at its center (see below). It is also known as *tripura (tri* - three, *pura* - worlds). It represents the three aspects of consciousness: cognition, conation, affection; the three modes of experience: knowing, doing, and feeling; and the three divinities: Brahma, Vishnu, and Shiva. Bright red in color, it is the point of origin of many Nadis such as the Ida, Pingala, Sushumna, Saraswati, Chitra, and Vajrini. The downward-pointing triangle is also called the *yoni* (female generative organ) and *kamakhya* or *kamaksha.* As *yoni* it is the abode of powers. As *kamakhya* it is the seat of desire. Kama and Kandarpa are two names of the lord of erotics. The vital force in the form of *kandarpa vayu,* the energy of pleasurable desires, is present in this triangle. An aspect of *apana vayu,* it is of the nature of fire and controls the desires of the embodied consciousness.

Svayambhu Lingam and Kundalini: *Svayam* means "self" and *bhu* means "originate," so *svayambhu* means "self-born." *Lingam* is generally used to mean "phallus," but in Sanskrit it also means "symbol," and it is said: *sarva bhut atmakam lingam,* "whatever exists is *lingam." Ling* means "gender" and is a symbol of the masculine form of energy. As such, it also is understood as Shiva, representing the male principle.

Kundalini represents the female principle. She is shown here in the form of a serpent coiled three and a half times around the Svayambhu Lingam. Her mouth is open in Sushumna (facing upward) and is connected with the Brahma Nadi.

She belongs to eternal consciousness *(vidya tattva* or *brahma vidya)* and is endowed with supreme yoga power. She is supremely subtle and is in deep desire for union with her beloved Lord, the Supreme Being.

The male and female principles, Shiva and Shakti (Kundalini), are together in the downward-pointing triangle *(tripura)* but not in complete union. Their union comes only in the Kameshvara Chakra (described in detail in the section on the Soma Chakra). The Lingam shines like lightning and the energy radiated by it is cool like a full moon, while the energy of Kundalini Shakti is hot and fire-like. Thus they are the eternal pair of opposites. The Lingam is black, which becomes shining gray because of the radiation emitting from it. It is described as *shyamala* (black, gray, greenish black). According to some scriptures, it has the color of a new green leaf, and the Kundalini Shakti that wraps around it is dark green in color. The aspirant should meditate on Shiva and Shakti as the Lingam and coiled serpent which radiate like the moon and sun.

The *Rudrayamala Tantra* states that the Svayambhu Lingam shines like ten million suns. It is the source of all knowledge and cannot be reached by intellectual knowledge. It is revealed only by true knowledge *(tattvajnana)* and deep concentration *(dhyana)*. The aspirant can see this Lingam only when he or she becomes conscious of the true nature of the Self which is beyond physical and psychological existence. Then the spiritual Self is born within *(svayambhu)*.

Element *(Tattva)*: Earth is the densest of all the elements, being the mixture of the four other elements: water, fire, air, and *akasha*. It gives stability and security and provides conditions for human completion on all levels. The sense of smell is related to the element earth and the nose is the sense organ of this chakra. Earth dominates the body chemistry for 20 minutes when breath flows from the right or left nostril. The element earth (not the planet) is the foundation of the body, the bones, flesh, skin, Nadis, and body hairs. Their growth is enhanced by the earth element when it becomes dominant during the nasal breathing from one of the two nostrils. It is best suited for stationary activities as it gives persistence. The sweet tasting earth element in conjunction with water forms the *kapha* (mucus) *dosha,* one of the three bodily humors described by the Indian science of medicine, Ayurveda. Worship done in the presence of this element brings *siddhis* (supernatural powers).

Seed Sound (Bija Mantra): The seed sound *LANG* is produced by putting the lips in a square shape and pushing the tongue in a square shape against the palate. The sound vibrates the palate, the brain, and the top of the cranium.

When properly produced, the sound *LANG* excites the Nadis in the first chakra and creates a lock that prevents the downward movement of energy. The upward movement of energy starts when the end of the sound, *ANG,* vibrates the upper head. *LA* is the earth and *NG* is *nada-bindu,* the primal cosmic sound from which the universe manifested. Repetition of the *bija mantra* deepens concentration, giving awareness and inner strength. Its vibrations help to create a passage inside the Brahma Nadi. They are absorbed in the Kundalini Shakti, which, when aroused, flows through the Brahma Nadi in the Sushumna path. The mantra becomes live energy which takes away the insecurities associated with the first chakra.

LANG is connected with the element earth and its presiding deity Indra. That is why it is called the *aindra-bija. LANG* is also called *prithvi-bija* and *kshiti-bija* (*prithvi* and *kshiti* mean "earth"). It arouses the power of Indra and assumes the form of the deity with four arms mounted on the elephant Airavata.

Carrier (Vahana) of the Seed Sound: The elephant Airavata is one of the fourteen gems which came from the churning of the ocean. Indra, the lord of the firmament, selected it as his vehicle. Traditionally Airavata is shown as a white elephant with seven trunks. The seven trunks are the colors of the rainbow (violet, indigo, blue, green, yellow, orange, and red—the seven different frequencies of light). These seven frequencies represent the seven aspects of individual consciousness that must be recognized and that evolved in harmony with natural laws. The rainbow is naturally associated with Indra, who, as lord of the firmament, is also the god of rain and thunder. Indra is the chief of the sub-gods, implying one who has mastered his sense organs and work organs *(indriyas).* The seven types of desires (for security, sexuality, longevity, sharing, knowledge, self-realization, and union) are also seen in the seven trunks and seven colors. They are associated with the seven chakras, the seven notes in an octave, and seven major planets.

The elephant is a symbol of strength. Physical strength comes from the seven constituents of the physical body *(dhatus),* which are nourished on a cellular level by the earth element:

- *Raja* – earth, clay
- *Rasa* – fluids
- *Rakta* – blood
- *Mansa* – flesh, nerves, fibers, tissues
- *Medha* – fat
- *Asthi* – bones
- *Majjan* – bone marrow

The elephant represents the fundamental urge for survival, a lifelong search for food for the body, the mind, and the heart. Because the elephant can carry heavy loads, it is a symbol of physical strength. Yet the elephant also carries out the orders of its master with humility, indicating that physical development need not impede spiritual growth but can harmonize with spiritual qualities. Airavata, a white elephant, represents spiritualized physical development. *Kunjara* or *Ganesh Kriya* (rinsing the anal region with water with the help of a finger) was developed from the elephant's example. It is used in Yoga for purification and vitalization of the body (lower abdominal tract) and makes the aspirant fit for practice of adamantine control. On the psychophysical level, a well-worked-out first chakra brings self control, physical strength, patience, the ability to bear heavy workloads, and a disciplined life.

Deity: Brahma. The lord of creation, Brahma, rules the direction North and is *sattvik* (pure, clear) in nature. Brahma's *sattvik* energy appears during the twilight hours of dawn and dusk. By envisioning him, one invokes a peaceful stillness in the mind. All fears and insecurities are resolved through Lord Brahma, the ever-watchful creator. The basic aspect of the Brahma-form is the smell principle *(gandha tanmatra).* In his unmanifest state he is within the *bindu,* the supreme truth which is the seed of all manifest phenomenon. It is said that before manifestation the creative power assumes a three-fold character, the three specific power points of *bindu, bija,* and *nada (Sharda Tilak).* The bursting of the *bindu* is the beginning of differentiation. Brahma, the creator of the physical plane (Bhu Loka), emerges from the *bindu*. When creation starts, *bindu* becomes *bija* and then *nada*. From *bija* comes Vishnu, and from *nada* emerges Rudra.

When the seed sound *LANG* is repeated with breath flowing in the earth element at the first chakra, Brahma manifests as a child, Bal Brahma (*bal* - child) who shines like the morning sun. This radiant Child Brahma has four heads and four arms. His skin is the color of wheat. He wears a yellow *dhoti* (traditional Indian cloth wrapped to cover the lower body), a green scarf, and a sacred thread. Each of Brahma's four hands carries a blessing for the aspirant. With one he is granting fearlessness *(abhai mudra)* and boons. The second hand holds a water pot *(kamandalu),* which carries the sacred water, the elixir. In his third hand is a lotus flower or a rosary *(mala)* for *japa*. In his fourth hand he carries scrolls depicting the divine knowledge. With four heads, he sees in all four directions at the same time. Each head represents one of the four aspects of human consciousness. These are recognized as:

1. The Physical Self: The cellular body which survives on food, sleep, and sex and needs exercise to grow and develop. The physical self is manifested through earth, matter, and the mother energy.

2. The Rational Self: The intellectual or conditioned logic of an individual's reasoning process.

3. The Emotional Self: The moods and sentiments that shift continually within the person. Loyalties and romance are influenced by the emotional self through electro-chemical energy.

4. The Intuitive Self: The inner voice of the person's conscious mind.

The four faces or heads of Brahma also represent the four forms of sound:

- ❧ *Para* – unmanifested or causal.
- ❧ *Pashyanti* – manifested as primal vibrations, *pranava*.
- ❧ *Madhyama* – clearly defined, organized, finds tone, voice.
- ❧ *Vaikhari* – audible acoustic dialogue.

Through these four heads, Brahma imparts cosmic wisdom as four *Vedas* (sacred scriptures). When Brahma is invoked by the repetition of *LANG,* all four aspects of the aspirant's consciousness are brightened by the luster of Brahma.

Shakti: Dakini. The word *dakini* comes from *dhatu,* which means "the beholder." She is the presiding divinity, the doorkeeper, and the power or energy *(shakti)* of the Muladhara Chakra. Entrance into the path of Sushumna is not possible without pleasing the doorkeeper. Dakini should be worshipped as Shakti of Brahma (power of Brahma). Her color is radiant pink, her eyes are shining red. In the *Gandharva Tantra* her color is described as being white and in *Khat Chakra Nirupana* she is described as splendorous, like the brilliance of many suns rising simultaneously. Although in *Koulavali Tantra* she is described as being red like the rising sun and having fierce teeth—an angry-looking, fearsome goddess—she should be visualized in her pleasant mood and form for meditation.

Dakini carries the light of divine knowledge which she imparts to yogis. Her single head indicates concentration, in which I-consciousness dissolves. *Kankalmalini Tantra* describes her face as beautiful as the moon. *Kularnava Tantra* says she is radiant and appears agile. She is divinely dressed and is the mother of wealth. She has four arms and hands. In her lower right hand she holds a sword with which she removes fear, destroys ignorance, and helps the aspirant *(sadhaka)* surmount all difficulties. In her upper right hand she holds a shield for protection. In her lower left hand she holds a skull (sometimes a skulled staff), which indicates detachment from the fear of death, the basic psychological block of the first chakra. In her upper left hand she holds a trident which symbolizes the combined energy of the creator, the preserver, and the destroyer.

Ruler: Ganesha. The elephant-headed god, Ganesha, is the lord to be invoked at the beginning of all undertakings to bestow protection and remove all obstacles. Ganesha was created by the Divine Mother Shakti, the consort of Shiva, from the clay *(raja)* of her own body. This story of his birth demonstrates his clear connection with the earth element *(raja)* of the first chakra. Thus, at the beginning of all ceremonies from birth to death, including the meditation on Kundalini, a piece of clay symbolizing Ganesha should be worshipped first. (Additional details of the story of Ganesha are given my book *Tools for Tantra.*)

Ganesha's skin color is coral orange. He wears a *dhoti* of lemon yellow color. A green silk scarf drapes his shoulders. He has four arms to serve him while he acts as the destroyer of obstacles. In his upper right hand he holds a hatchet symbolizing control of the "elephant of desires" and the cutting away of the bondage of desires. The hatchet cuts the person away from the false identification of his or her true Self with the physical body. With his lower right hand Ganesha grants fearlessness.

His upper left hand holds a lasso *(pash),* symbolizing the bondage of worldly attachment. His lower left hand holds a *laddu,* a fragrant sweet ball made of chickpea flour, which symbolizes *sattva,* the most refined state of pure consciousness. The *laddu* also brings health and prosperity to the household.

The rational mind creates obstacles to worship of any kind. Worship of Ganesha involves accepting him as a remover of obstacles. This subdues the rational mind, or the left hemisphere, which is analytical and critical in nature, and frees the right hemisphere, which is emotional and which is needed for any spiritual venture. Visualization of Ganesha helps in stopping the internal dialogue. One who is put off by the external form cannot admire the internal beauty and power of Ganesha, but one who penetrates the physical reality can see in Ganesha the union of love and wisdom.

Techniques and Effects of Meditation: Meditation on the tip of the nose (the sense organ of the Muladhara Chakra) induces awareness, freedom from disease, inspiration, vitality, vigor, stamina, endurance, stability, security, and lightness (the power of levitation). One achieves understanding of inner purity, softness in voice, and the power to hear inner melody *(nada).*

One who knows this chakra goes beyond darkness. The knowledge of the world arises from the Muladhara Chakra and it also is absorbed there. When the spiritual energy of Kundalini Shakti is aroused, it is radiant like a cluster of lights. By doing a special *kumbhaka* (holding of breath) in the Muladhara Chakra (which can be learned only from a guru), the body shakes and becomes light. The yogi starts dancing (levitating) and the universe in its subtle form is seen by the yogi. When the Ida and Pingala Nadis are controlled through *kumbhaka* and Kundalini starts to rise up in the Brahma Nadi, the gate of Brahman (Brahma Dvara) opens up. When Kundalini attains the highest position (*Yogashikhopanishad,* 6-22-34), the aspirant becomes free of worldliness and the true knowledge of the three worlds is attained.

Behavioral Characteristics in the Muladhara Chakra: This chakra encompasses the planes of genesis, illusion, anger, greed, delusion, avarice, and sensuality.

The energy in the first chakra is influenced by the earth element, and the earth element is connected with the desire for security in the form of job and shelter. A person who is dominated by the Muladhara Chakra is obsessed by the desire to find security.

Generally we can compare the behavior of first-chakra persons to the behavior of ants, which faithfully and egolessly work for the queen. Their ego is attached to gaining the favor of their boss. They are God-fearing and follow the laws of the institution for which they work. They are the foundation of the institution to which they belong, its *mul* (basic) *adhara* (support). They work hard, mostly for food and shelter. For them, food is to satisfy their hunger, not for taste.

Like the element earth they are solid and strong, endure all kinds of hardships, and are productive. They rely primarily on their muscles, bones, and nerves, which belong to the earth element. The use of food that is old, packaged, stale, and heavy *(tamasik)* makes them somewhat heavy and lethargic. They have no direction and need help in making decisions. They can follow orders without any hitch or difficulty, but cannot order others effectively. First-chakra persons are attracted to the worship of ghosts and awesome deities. They love rewards and are scared of punishment. They are humble and respectful to their boss or officers, but harsh to their subordinates and tough on their colleagues. When a first-chakra person enters the race of competition, he or she succeeds through physical strength, muscle power, endurance, and vigor. Greed becomes the main problem.

Normally a child from the ages of one to seven years acts out of first-chakra motivations. The earth is being grasped as a new experience. The infant must ground himself or herself. Mother and father are symbols of security. The young child will be self-centered and highly concerned with his or her own physical survival. Playing with earth and clay, building toy houses, and eating sweets (the taste of the element earth) are very appealing to this age group.

It is difficult but necessary for a child to learn to regulate patterns of eating, drinking, and sleeping. The child will learn good behavior, such as paying proper respect to others, if the parents become strict but remains loving. However, children become resentful if they are asked all the time not to do this or that. They learn more easily by imitating, so the best way of teaching is to provide a good example.

When there is a threat to his or her security, a child or a first-chakra person can become violent, causing many problems. A fearful person may strike out blindly and senselessly, like a cornered animal, due to what is felt to be a loss of basic *(mula)* security. Tightened jaws and fists are their usual stance when they are surrounded by various kinds of people. Strength is their best friend and weakness of any kind their worst enemy.

Persons dominated by this chakra generally sleep between ten and twelve hours nightly on their stomach, eat more, talk less, are mindless or absent minded, and do not live according to natural laws (are not health food conscious). They should be introduced to better ways of living and eating which will reduce their fear. Like children, they need guidance.

Muladhara Chakra is the seat of the coiled Kundalini and is the root of all growth and awareness of human divinity. However, when this chakra becomes a hang-up that prevents energy from flowing in higher centers, it makes one very self-centered, cruel, and violent. It can make people become criminals or lead them to take jobs such as that of a soldier or policeman where they act out their basic problems and, by virtue of the authority vested in them, be violent and cruel without being criminals. The only cure is to follow the *yamas* and *niyamas* (restraints and practices) and live in accordance with natural laws, having food, sleep, and sex in moderation. One should practice *pranayama* (the control of *prana*) and keep the physical system free from foul smells which make the *apana* more toxic.

SVADHISHTHANA CHAKRA
(SECOND CHAKRA)

Names:	Svadhishthana, Adhishthan, Shaddala
Meanings of the Names:	Dwelling Place of the Self (*sva* – self or *prana, adhisthana* – dwelling place), Six-Petaled
Location:	Genital region, hypogastric plexus
Element *(Tattva):*	Water
Color of the Element:	Color of water: transparent, white, light blue
Shape *(Yantra)* of the Element:	Circle, like a drop of water
Seed Sound *(Bija Mantra)* of the Element:	*VANG*
Color of the Seed Sound:	Gold
Carrier *(Vahana)* of the Seed Sound:	Crocodile *(makara)*
Number of Petals:	Six
Color of the Petals:	Red, vermilion with a touch of carmine
Seed Sounds of the Petals:	*BANG, BHANG, MANG, YANG, RANG, LANG*
Aspects:	Procreation, family, fantasy, creativity, sensuality
Predominant Sense:	Taste
Sense Organ:	Tongue
Work Organ:	Genitals
Air *(Vayu, Prana):*	*Apana* (see description in first chakra)
Plane *(Loka):*	Astral plane *(Bhuvar Loka)*
Ruling Planet:	Mercury (lunar, feminine)

Yantra **Form:** The circle with crescent. The circle, representing the element water, is to be colored white. The crescent inside the circle is associated with the moon and so it is colored silver.

The combination of the crescent moon with the circle in the yantra of the Svadhishthana Chakra clearly establishes the relationship between water and the moon. The moon by itself is related to the Soma Chakra and is not the ruling planet of the Svadhishthana Chakra. However, the moon plays a great role in the

Svadishthana Chakra

स्वाधिष्ठान् चक्र

Bija petal sound

बं भंमं यंरंलं

life of a second-chakra person who goes through many emotional fluctuations during the changing phases of the moon. Because the Svadhishthana Chakra is associated with the genitals, it is connected with procreation, which is directly related to the moon. The menstrual cycle of women mirrors the monthly cycle of the moon.

The Circle with Six Petals: Outside the white circle representing the element are six lotus petals. The color of these petals is a deeper red than that of the petals of Muladhara Chakra. It is a mixture of vermilion with deep red (carmine or scarlet). The six petals represent six important mental modifications *(vritties)*: (1) affection (indulgence), (2) suspicion, (3) disdain, (4) delusion, (5) destructiveness, and (6) pitilessness (as stated in the *Mahanirvana Tantra*). These mental modifications are the energies of the divinities connected with the petals.

Element *(Tattva)*: Water is life-giving and it is called the essence of life. Three-fourths of the earth is covered with water, and almost three-fourths of the weight of the human body is water, which is present as blood, mucus, urine, saliva, lymph, and other fluids. The water element evolves from the *rasa tanmatra* (taste principle), which is why the tongue is its sense organ. Water is intimately connected with the moon, which is shown by the influence of the lunar cycle on ocean tides. The waxing and waning of the moon also influences our body chemistry and our emotions. The water element is also connected to the moon in our breathing cycle. Lunar energy is evoked when the water element (which is dominant for 16 minutes in each nasal breath cycle of one hour) is accompanied by breathing dominated by the left nostril. Left nostril breathing activates the Ida Nadi, which is lunar in nature. When the Ida Nadi is activated, it stimulates the right hemisphere of the brain, which is related to emotional behavior. Thus, in this chakra, we see the relationship between water, the moon, emotions, and the psyche.

Seed Sound *(Bija Mantra)*: *VANG*. To produce this sound, the lips are shaped like a circle and air is pushed through the lips with the sound resonating as if it is coming from a tube. The concentration should be on the image of the second chakra (not the genitals) when the seed sound *VANG* is repeated. If produced properly, the sound of this *bija mantra* will influence the flow of *prana* in the Svadhishthana Chakra. Water sounds enhance the power of this seed sound: when the *bija mantra* is repeated in the presence of the water element it enhances the production and circulation of fluids in the body. The power of Varuna, an aspect of Vishnu, is present in the *bija mantra VANG.* When it is repeated in conjunction with the seed sounds of the six petals *(BANG, BHANG, MANG,YANG, RANG, and LANG),* the chakra energy is purified and is able to clear away many blocks in the lower regions of the body.

Carrier *(Vahana)* of the Seed Sound: Crocodile *(makara).* The crocodile represents sexual vigor. It is an animal that moves with a serpentine motion, depicting the sensuous nature of the second-chakra person. The fat of the crocodile was once used to increase virility in men. The crocodile captures its prey through many tricks. It enjoys floating and diving deep beneath the water. The crocodile's habits of hunting, trickery, sunbathing on beaches, floating, and fantasizing are qualities of a person obsessed by a second-chakra mind. The English saying "to shed crocodile tears" is also known in Indian languages, and refers to a false display of emotions. The crocodile is the vehicle of Varuna, the lord of water in ocean, rivers, lakes, and ponds. Varuna is related to Indra, the lord of the water in rain and clouds, who is associated with the first chakra. Similarly, the sexual energy of the second chakra is related to the energy of the first chakra—the desire for food for the body, mind, and heart. The air *(vayu)* of both chakras is *apana.* Therefore, a strong first chakra enhances sexual play in the second chakra.

Deity: Vishnu, the lord of preservation. Brahma creates, but after creation comes preservation. Preservation is aided by the vital life force *(prana)* and several energies that operate together to help the organism grow and flourish. These life-giving energies are different divinities that reside inside the body. All these gods and sub-gods are Vishnu-energy. Vishnu is the source of the highest spiritual power and knowledge that is present in every atom and cell. The word *vishnu* comes from *vish* which means "pervasion." He pervades all. The universe is maintained by his power. When everything is destroyed in the dissolution *(pralaya),* only Vishnu remains. He is the god who is responsible for maintaining an equilibrium between the life-giving forces of Brahma and the destructive forces of Shiva. Whenever the balance is disturbed between the forces of creation and destruction, Vishnu has to incarnate to create a balance again. He is the eternal benefactor of the Svadhishthana Chakra.

Vishnu's skin is cerulean blue and he wears a *dhoti* of golden yellow. A green scarf covers his four arms. Vishnu is sometimes shown as being dark blue or black, riding his concentrated *vayu* power in the form of Garuda (the eagle, the king of the birds). When the *sattvik* aspect of Vishnu is depicted, he is colored crystal-white. In that form he is called Satya Narayan and represents the never-changing truth *(satya)* inside everything, the eternal formless. Vishnu, the eternal supreme truth, wears a garland made of wild flowers *(van mala)* that is ever-changing illusion *(maya)*. The *apana vayu* which is also present, is *rajasik* in quality. Thus the dark blue color of Vishnu, influenced by the yellow color of *rajas,* appears sea-green or turquoise-blue in color.

In his four arms Vishnu holds four implements that are essential for the full enjoyment of life through accomplishment of the four *padarthas* (objects of achievement): wealth *(artha)*, code of conduct or law *(dharma)*, enjoyment of beauty *(kama)*, and liberation *(moksha)*.

- ℭ *Gada,* the mace or club, symbolizes the power to control. The mace is a tool to break through obstacles. It is made of metal, which is earth and its color is metallic silver. When Vishnu is depicted as holding it in his lower right hand, it means that the control of earth and its immense wealth are in his power. Through his *gada,* Vishnu has the power of maintaining the world. It also signifies that earthly security in the form of monetary wealth *(artha)* is the first requirement before sexual desires *(kama)* can be fulfilled.

- ℭ *Chakra* is the golden ring of light (consciousness), spinning on the index finger of Vishnu's upper right hand. In continuous movement around its axis, staying firm and true to its revolution, it symbolizes *dharma,* natural law. This wheel of *dharma (dharma chakra)* revolves on the axis of the power of preservative energy. Its steady revolution creates the cycle of time, the cosmic rhythm, the dance of preservation *(rasa lila)*. Whatever is not in conformity with this cosmic rhythm must automatically come to an end. The *chakra* cuts through obstacles such as ignorance and irreverence and destroys disharmony and imbalance.

- ℭ *Padma,* the lotus of pale pink color held in Vishnu's left hand, is a symbol of purity. A lotus grows in the mud, yet remains luminous, radiant, and graceful, completely unaffected by its environment. The lotus is also a symbol of beauty and the enjoyment of beauty *(kama)*.

ന *Shankh,* the conch shell, contains the sound of ocean waves and represents the pure sound *(mantra)* that brings liberation *(moksha)* to human beings. The conch is the principle of the void *(akasha)*. Its color is white.

Vishnu embodies the principles of right living. His nature is that of *lila* (play, divine sport). He is also the hero of the cosmic drama. All this should be kept in mind while meditating on Vishnu.

Shakti: Rakini. The two-headed Rakini is the doorkeeper of the Svadhishthana Chakra. The two heads of Rakini represent the split energy of the second chakra. They indicate the duality between "I" and the other. The efforts and energy of the second-chakra person are spent on attaining a balance between the world without and the world within. Like Dakini of the Muladhara Chakra, Rakini is an aspect of Kundalini Shakti. Her skin is pale pink or red (as stated in the *Kankalmalini Tantra*). However, other Tantric scriptures like *Kularnava* and *Tantra Khat Chakra Nirupana* describe her color as being like the color of the dark blue lotus, black, lustrous, and frightful with prominent teeth. She wears a red sari and jewels encircle her neck and four arms. Her scarf is light and dark blue. Her face is beautiful, delightful, and inspiring to those who follow restraint in gratifying their desires; she is awesome and frightful to those who are slaves of their desires. The first inspiration of art and music comes from Rakini Shakti.

In her four arms Rakini holds the following implements:

ന An arrow. Shot from the bow of Kama, the lord of erotic love, this arrow depicts the concentration of desire upon its object. Desire can make a person one-pointed by keeping energy from flowing in many directions. But such one-pointedness is not a permanent feature of the character of a second-chakra person. It persists only as long as the arrow does not hit the desired target. The arrow also indicates the impetus for upward movement within this chakra. The arrow of Rakini is the arrow of feelings and emotions that bring both pleasure and pain as duality arises.

- A skull. The skull symbolizes the nature of the romantic, who bears his head on his hand, with emotions ruling his behavior. It also indicates freedom from the fear of death, which adds to the romantic nature of a second-chakra person.

- A drum *(damaru)*. The drum represents sound *(mantra)* and rhythm. It is said that at the time of creation Shiva, in a joyful mood, played his drum from which came the 16 vowels and 34 consonants of the Sanskrit language known as *matrikas* (mother energy expressed as sound). The sound of the *damaru* thus signifies *nada*, or *mantra*. The beating of the drum also marks time and the rhythm cycle. Rhythm makes the body move in dance form, and dance is a powerful tool of expression for the second-chakra person.

- An ax *(parashu)*. The ax symbolizes removal of deeply rooted unspiritual qualities. The ax is a most ancient tool, if not the first. With it, Rakini Shakti cuts through all the obstacles within the second chakra that block the path of further growth of the personality.

Techniques and Effects of Meditation: Meditation on the Svadhishthana Chakra enables the mind to reflect the world as the moon reflects the sun. One acquires the ability to use creative and sustaining energy to elevate oneself to refined arts and pure relationships with others, having become free of lust, anger, greed, unsettledness, and jealousy. It combines meditation on the element water as the essence of life, on *apana vayu* as the vital life force, on the petals, on Vishnu, and on Rakini. Aspirants should meditate on the six petals and repeat their *bija mantras*. Loud *japa* in melodious tones can be done when one is coloring the petals, and silent repetition can be done during the visualization exercise. While chanting the seed sounds one should concentrate on the *uddiyana bandha* described on page 53 in chapter 2, "Kundalini and Yoga." If regularly practiced, *uddiyana bandha* helps in the restoration of sexual functioning and the control of abdominal muscles and the bladder during *kumbhaka* (holding the breath). This allows an unobstructed flow of energy with *apana vayu*. If the meditation on the second chakra is done in the presence of the water element, it leads to *bhakti*, emotional involvement with any of the forms of the Divine, especially Vishnu, who pervades all forms. It clears the passage of spiritual energy beyond the Brahma Granthi, the knot of the world of names and forms.

When Lord Vishnu, who is beneficent with a countenance of the purest nature, is visualized, a feeling of peacefulness ensues, as still as a lake. Meditation on Rakini enables her arrow to cut through the mental modifications of suspicion, disdain, delusion, pitilessness, and destructiveness that occupy the petals of this chakra. Meditation on the second chakra also increases personal magnetism, refinement in behavior, freedom from diseases of the body, and longevity. Worldly pleasures and treasures are given up for the sake of one's beloved. The beloved becomes one's world and the world outside disappears. This detachment from the world helps the aspirant of yoga to follow the upward movement of energy. Truth becomes love and love is God.

Behavioral Characteristics in the Svadhishthana Chakra: Svadhishthana Chakra encompasses the astral plane, the space between heaven and earth, as well as the planes of entertainment, fantasy, nullity, jealousy, mercy, and joy (in the company of the opposite sex only). The energy in the Svadhishthana Chakra is influenced by the water element. Water is connected with life as shown by the Sanskrit word for life *(jivan),* which also means water. As this chakra is connected with the procreation of life, it is also related with family and the responsibilities of a family. The genitals being its work organ, it is connected with sexuality and fantasies.

The expansion of personality starts in this chakra. In the first chakra the personality revolved around the employer, employment, and colleagues. In the second chakra the circle of friends widens. The person tries to establish his or her identity to attract members of the opposite sex. Self-glorification starts and admirers are needed. High ideals are attractive. Sacrifices for others (of the opposite sex exclusively) begins. This is very beautifully realized in marriage and family life. As long as one remains true to the norms of family life there are no problems in the second chakra, but when one attaches too much importance to sense gratification and becomes selfish then this chakra creates psychological problems.

In the first chakra the basic goals were to pursue monetary security and muscle power. The attention was linear and followed a single direction. In the second chakra the attention is diverted to desires, fantasies of a sexual nature, and creativity.

Art, music, and poetry are attractive and meaningful. Here the earth becomes a jewel and heaven is within reach. A sense of taste develops and food is not only to satisfy hunger but also for enjoyment. A second-chakra person seeks occasions of amusement, visits clubs and parties, partakes in competitions, and seeks the attention of members of opposite sex. He or she will sleep eight to ten hours nightly in a fetal position.

Imagination, fantasies, and moods cause the behavior of a second-chakra person to change constantly. Desire, which basically is creative desire, culminates in the desire for love, in which the senses function in relation to pleasurable objects and the conative organs (the mind, intellect, ego, and feeling self) heighten the feelings of pleasure. In this chakra, the desire for the highest enjoyment, the bliss attained in *samadhi,* takes the form of a longing for conjugal pleasure. Excitement is sought in physical beauty, rhythmic movement, thrilling music, nudes and stories and poems heralding royal heroes and heroines, destroyers of evil. The media provide lots of material for excitement and enjoyment for the second-chakra person. As first-chakra people believe in ghosts and evil spirits, second-chakra persons believe in superstitions, omens, and the influences of dreams.

A second-chakra person often pretends to be a prince or princess, hero or heroine, changes roles, maintains a high self-esteem, and is chivalrous. The behavior of a second-chakra person can be called the way of the butterfly—enjoying every beautiful flower, flirting, flying, forgetting. There is more fun in waiting than in mating. Shedding crocodile tears is common second-chakra behavior.

Normally a person between the ages of eight and fourteen acts from second-chakra motivation. Like earth dissolving into water, the child begins to reach out to his family and friends for physical contact, instead of standing alone and defensive, as he did in the first chakra. The imagination increases. Once the need for food and shelter is met, the person is free to visualize any environment and circumstance that he or she desires. Sexuality enters into relationships as a new awareness of the physical body evolves. Rules and regulations of the family and society become unbearable and one becomes a rebel.

The second chakra also includes nullity, a state of emptiness and purposelessness. When the world is seen as an obstacle, social laws as restrictions, and discipline as unwanted control, the negative mind starts working. Nothing excites, nothing pleases, pessimism takes over, and suicidal tendencies develop. Envy and jealousy arise from the desire to possess the time or qualities of others. This results in states of restlessness, anxiety, and destructiveness. The desire for physical sensation and mental fantasies can also cause a problem for the person at this level. Inventing stories to get attention, telling lies, false self-esteem and keeping bad company can cause strain. Just as water flows from higher levels to lower levels, the second chakra can have a downward whirlpool effect on the psyche. If the person is to remain healthy and balanced, the natural limitations of the body and mind must be understood and respected. Eating, sleeping, and sex must be regulated in order to attain a harmonious, peaceful state.

In the first chakra sexual enjoyment is to satisfy physical urges and for grounding. In the second chakra it becomes enjoyable by itself and, if they are not spiritual, these persons go in for sexual excesses. In the third chakra sex gives release from tensions and a sense of authority and control. In the fourth chakra sex is company, touch. In the fifth chakra sexual satisfaction comes through sound. In every chakra sex is enjoyed but in the second chakra it needs all of the following aspects: satisfaction of the physical urge, playful games with different body positions *(asanas),* control, touch, and sound. If the person is spiritual, sex remains confined to one partner, but the mind remains occupied with the physical body more than the person inside the body.

SPECIAL NOTE: Left-handed Tantra offers a way of elevating consciousness to the highest level of *samadhi* through sexual rites. It is known as "yoga through *bhoga* (enjoyment)." By using sexual energy to excite spiritual energy, left-handed Tantric practices subdue the restless mind and make it one-pointed. Sexual intercourse *(maithuna)* is used as a device to arouse the coiled Kundalini Shakti. *Apana* control techniques are used to restrain the *kandarpa vayu* and stop ejaculation. Instead, the seminal fluid, with the vaginal fluid, is directed upward to Soma Chakra.

MANIPURA CHAKRA
(THIRD CHAKRA)

Names:	Manipura, Manipurak, Nabhi
Meanings of the Names:	City of Jewels or Gems (*mani* - jewel or gem, *pura* - dwelling place), Navel (*nabhi* - navel)
Location:	The part of the vertebral column that corresponds to the navel region
Element *(Tattva):*	Fire
Color of the Element:	Red, like fire or the rising sun
Shape *(Yantra)* of the Element:	Triangle (downward-pointing)
Seed Sound *(Bija Mantra)* of the Element:	*RANG*
Color of the Seed Sound:	Gold
Carrier *(Vahana)* of the Seed Sound:	Ram *(mesha)*
Number of Petals:	Ten
Color of the Petals:	Blue
Seed Sounds of the Petals:	*DANG, DHANG, RLANG* (palatal sounds); *TANG, THANG, DANG, DHANG* (dental sounds); *NANG, PANG, PHANG* (labial sounds)
Aspects:	Vision, form, color, ego
Predominant Sense:	Sight
Sense Organ:	Eyes
Work Organ:	Feet and legs
Air *(Vayu, Prana):*	*Saman,* the air that dwells in the upper abdominal region in the area of the navel, helping the digestive system to produce, assimilate and distribute the essence of food to the entire body
Plane *(Loka):*	Celestial plane *(Sva or Svarga Loka)*
Ruling Planet:	Sun (solar, masculine)

Yantra **Form:** Inverted triangle that is fiery red in color. The triangle is the symbol for the fire element. Through this element, manifested energy is given a form (*rupa*). The triangle is the simplest rigid geometric form: it needs only three sides,

Manipura Chakra

मणिपूर चक्र

Bija petal sound

डंढंणंतंथंदंधं नं पं फं

and yet it is an entity in itself. The inverted triangle suggests the movement of energy downward. It obstructs the upward movement of Kundalini until it is pierced. Visualization of the triangle of bright red color helps the aspirant in his or her spiritual evolution. The first knot, Brahma Granthi, is also found in the Manipura Chakra.

The Circle with Ten Petals: The red triangle is located inside a circle surrounded by ten lotus petals. Each petal represents one aspect of Braddha Rudra (Old Shiva), the deity of this chakra. They are the seat of ten mental modifications *(vritties):* (1) spiritual ignorance *(avidya),* (2) thirst *(trishna),* (3) jealousy *(dvesh),* (4) treachery *(krurta),* (5) shame *(lajja),* (6) fear *(bhai),* (7) disgust *(nirasha),* (8) delusion *(bhrama),* (9) foolishness *(murkhta),* and (10) sadness *(udasinta, dukha).* The ten petals also depict the ten pranas *(prana, apana, samana, vyana, udana, naag, dhananjaye, devdutta, kurma,* and *krikil).*

The color of the petals is blue, like the blue flame of the most luminous part of a fire. *Khat Chakra Nirupana* states that they are the deep black color of dense rain clouds *(purna megh prakash)* but *Kankalmalini Tantra* and many other tantric scriptures accept blue as the color of the petals.

Element *(Tattva):* Fire is both heat and light energy, but heat is dominant. It is related to the sun, the ruling planet of this chakra. The sun is the source of life in the solar system, and the navel represents the source of life in the body. A child in the womb is connected with its mother through the umbilical cord which, when severed, becomes the navel. The mother is the source of nourishment and energy for the growing fetus. Fire is the form in which the Kundalini energy remains in the body. The fire in the navel region aids in the digestion and absorption of food, which supplies the whole body with the vital energy needed for survival. It is related to hunger, thirst, sleep, lethargy, and radiance *(ojas).* Fire is purifying and nourishing, yet it can also be destructive when it gets out of control.

The Sushumna Nadi is of the nature of fire. The right nostril (Pingala Nadi) is the sun, the left nostril (Ida Nadi) is the moon. When both nostrils work together, the Sushumna is activated. Energy flows in ten directions when the energy comes to the fire element for twelve minutes during each cycle of nasal breathing.

Seed Sound *(Bija Mantra):* *RANG.* This sound is produced by forming a triangular shape with the lips and pushing the tongue against the palate. The main point of concentration when producing this seed sound is on the third chakra. The sound originates from the navel when repeated in a proper manner. The sound *RANG* increases the digestive fire, which enhances assimilation and absorption. It contributes to longevity, the main goal of a person motivated by the third chakra. The nature of fire is to move upwards and the repetition *(japa)* of the mantra *RANG,* when produced properly, helps the upward movement of Kundalini. This *bija mantra* should be visualized as always seated in the downward-pointing triangle.

Carrier *(Vahana)* of the Seed Sound: The ram *(mesha)* is the carrier of the seed sound *RANG.* The ram is a vehicle of the fire god, Agni, and is also associated with the planet Mars. The ram depicts the nature of a third-chakra person. While sheep are famous for their group consciousness and peaceful, innocent nature, the ram is famous for physical strength and stamina in fighting. A fighter, it charges its opponents head-on and does not give up easily. The sound produced by blowing a ram's horn was used by soldiers in war to give them courage and fighting strength.

Deity: Braddha Rudra (Old Shiva). Rudra, the wrathful form of Shiva, rules the Southern direction and represents the power of destruction. Destruction of one cycle of creation is also the beginning of the next cycle. At the end of each cycle, all that exists returns to him. Rudra also implies weeping and lamentation because *rudra* comes from the Sanskrit root *rud* which means "crying."

Rudra is red with anger but he appears to be white or grayish-white because his body is smeared with ashes. Although Shiva's skin is camphor blue or red in other manifestations, Braddha Rudra should be meditated upon as an ash-colored deity. He has a shining white beard like a *rishi.* He is seated on a tiger skin smeared with ashes and is dressed in a tiger skin. The tiger represents the mind *(manas).* In his right hand he holds a trident and in his left hand a *damaru* (drum). He is not shown granting fearlessness or boons like other divinities, but meditation on him dispels fear and subsides anger. He is adorned with snakes and often a *rudraksha mala (rudraksha* - fruit, *mala* - rosary). Rudra should be meditated on seated inside the seed sound *RANG.*

Shakti: Lakini Devi, another form of Kundalini Shakti, is the doorkeeper of Manipura Chakra. She is also known as Bhadra Kali, the compassionate form of Kali. She has three faces, indicating that the scope of vision in the third chakra encompasses three planes, the physical, the astral, and the celestial. Her three heads also represent the mind *(manas)*, intellect *(buddhi)*, and I-consciousness *(ahamkara)*. Her color is orange red, peach red, or pink according to *Kankalmalini Tantra*, although in *Khat Chakra Nirupana* she is said to have a dark complexion, large teeth, and an awesome appearance. According to *Kankalmalini* Tantra she is beautiful like the moon, adorned with ornaments, with bright shining eyes that are painted with collyrium *(kajal)*. The color of her sari is said to be radiating light blue, even though the author of commentaries on the *Khat Chakra Nirupana* states that it is yellow.

Lakini has four arms. In her upper right hand she holds the fire of purification in a fire pot *(havan kund)*. It indicates the energy of fire as well as the physical heat that emanates from within the body *(vaishvanara agni* - body temperature). Her lower right hand forms the hand gesture of granting fearlessness and boons, *abhai mudra*. In her upper left hand she holds a thunder bolt *(vajra)* from which energy is always emanating. In her lower left hand she holds an arrow, which symbolizes the impetus for the upward movement of energy. An arrow has a goal, a target to be shot at. The arrow of the second chakra is shot from the bow of Kama, the lord of sexuality and sensuality. The arrow in the third chakra is shot by the desires for accomplishment, freedom, independence, and authority.

Techniques and Effects of Meditation: Meditation on the Manipura Chakra starts with concentration on the ten petals, chanting each of their mantras from *DANG* to *PHANG* as the petals are visualized. Then comes concentration on the downward-pointing red triangle of the fire element, along with the repetition of the seed sound of the element, *RANG*. Both form *(rupa)* and the fiery Sushumna are implied in this meditation. This is followed by concentration on the ram *(mesha)* as the carrier of the seed sound. After the ram, Lakini Devi should be concentrated upon as the doorkeeper to Manipura Chakra, which shines like a precious gem. She leads the aspirant to meditation on Braddha Rudra in his calm and pure form, the guru of all spiritual knowledge. Braddha Rudra absorbs all the cosmic principles by which an aspirant is bound to worldliness, which appear as Brahma Granthi (the knot of Brahma). Practice of concentration in the above order enables the aspirant to attain success in yoga by aiding the ascent of Kundalini to the fourth chakra, the Anahata Chakra.

The root cause of worldliness, the ego, is not very active in the first two chakras. The ego develops in the third chakra with the growth of the desire to be somebody who is recognized by others as special and the desire to be powerful and authoritative, a king of one's own domain. Manipura is "the city of jewels," and the owner of the city is the king who has undisputed authority over the body. Rudra destroys this false entity, the ego, by destroying the world. The ego does not want to die but true knowledge shows that there is no death. Death is only a change; change is eternal and happens within the body all the time.

The yogic *siddhi* of entering into another body *(par-kaya-pravesh)* is obtained by a yogi who meditates on the third chakra in the presence of the fire element. The word for intense spiritual discipline, *tapasya,* comes from the root *tap,* which means "temperature" or "to get heated by fire." Fire is a great purifier and *tapasya* makes one pure; egotism is overcome and one achieves the power to create and destroy the world. The *bija mantra RANG* increases the fire of Yoga *(yoga agni)* and gives the yogi the ability to walk on fire and play with fire.

Meditation on the third chakra brings an end to indigestion, constipation, and all problems of the intestinal region. Heat makes the blood thin so that it circulates better. Thus meditation on Manipura Chakra provides for a long, healthy life.

The fluidity given by the second chakra here assumes the form of practicality. The third chakra is governed by the sun, which rules over the intellect, as the moon rules the psyche. Fantasies are converted into practical devices through the help of the organizational power of this chakra. Through intellectual development, one achieves control over speech and can express ideas very effectively, giving one the power to command.

Behavioral Characteristics in the Manipura Chakra: This chakra encompasses the planes of karma, charity, atonement for one's errors, good company, bad company, selfless service, sorrow, *dharma,* and the celestial plane. It is the seat of the fire element, which manifests as angry looks, fiery temperament, and dashing personality. It is also the gravitational center of the body. The behavior of a third-chakra person is motivated by desires for identification, recognition, power, and better living conditions. Such a person will sleep from six to eight hours nightly on his or her back. The selfless loyalties of the first two chakras (to one's employer, family, and friends) cease, and the person acts only for himself or herself. Dissatisfaction kindles the fire and energy is consumed by egotistic pursuits of name and fame. Ambition and pride in achievement occupy a large part of the consciousness of third-chakra persons. Reputation, authority, and status are their main concerns. Second-chakra persons are intoxicated by youth, third-chakra persons by the desire for power. When aging brings the realization that the body will not last forever, they join organizations or create institutions to perpetuate their names.

As the Manipura Chakra is ruled by the sun, intellectual power plays an important role in the behavior of third-chakra persons. Like the ram, they walk with a proud air, as if drunk with vanity, and move towards their desired target without thinking about the consequences. They have great organizational abilities and, with the help of the intellect and power of expression, they are able to get a group of people to help them. They maintain control of others through anger, and behave like detached old persons.

Young persons between the ages of fourteen and twenty-one are generally ruled by the third chakra. They are very concerned about being fashionable and in tune with the time, with whatever is the latest. They demand respect from others and are arrogant inside and humble outside to gain favors and attention.

The ego is the main problem for this chakra. Although it exists in every chakra, the steering wheel of the ego changes. In the first chakra, it is steered by the employer, while in the second chakra, it is controlled by the opposite sex. In the third chakra, it becomes self-centered and strives for personal power, identification, and recognition, even to the detriment of family and friends. In the first chakra, the ego feels proud of muscular power; in the second chakra the ego feels proud of physical beauty, youth, and personal magnetism; in the third chakra the ego feels proud of the ability to control.

Balance in the Manipura Chakra can be achieved by selfless service, serving without desire for reward. Every person must be aware of his or her actions in order to achieve balance in life. Charity will clarify one's path of action or karma. *Dharma* is the timeless law of nature (inner and outer) that interconnects all phenomenal existence. By following the yogic path (Ashthanga Yoga) one can remain true to one's *dharma*, aiding relationships with others to become more stable and clear. After this balance is achieved, the person may enter the celestial plane, the plane of illumination.

Anahata Chakra

अनाहत् चक्र

Bija petal sound

कं खं गं घं ङं चं छं जं झं ञं टं ठं

ANAHATA CHAKRA
(FOURTH CHAKRA)

Names:	Anahata, Hritpankaja (in the *Khat Chakra Nirupana*), Dvadashadala (in the *Rudrayamala Tantra*)
Meanings of the Names:	Unstruck, Heart Lotus (*hrit* - heart, *pankaja* - lotus), Twelve-petaled (*dvadash* - twelve, *dala* - petals)
Location:	The heart region of the vertebral column, the cardiac plexus
Element *(Tattva):*	Air
Color of the Element:	Colorless, gray or smoky green
Shape *(Yantra)* of the Element:	Hexagram or six-pointed star
Seed Sound *(Bija Mantra)* of the Element:	*YANG*
Color of the Seed Sound:	Gold
Carrier *(Vahana)* of the Seed Sound:	Black antelope or musk deer
Number of Petals:	Twelve
Color of the Petals:	Deep red, vermilion
Seed Sounds of the Petals:	*KANG, KHANG, GANG, GHANG, YONG, CANG, CHANG, JANG, JHANG, UANG, TANG, THANG*
Aspects:	Balance
Predominant Sense:	Touch
Sense Organ:	Skin
Work Organ:	Hands
Air *(Vayu, Prana):*	*Prana,* the air that we breathe, rich in life-giving negative ions, dwelling in the chest region
Plane *(Loka):*	The plane of balance (*Maha Loka*)
Ruling Planet:	Venus (lunar, feminine)

Yantra **Form:** The hexagram or six-pointed star symbolizes the air element, which moves in all four directions as well as upward and downward. Air is the vital life-force (*prana*). It aids the functions of the lungs and the heart, circulating fresh oxygen and vital energy. The star is composed of two overlapping, intersecting triangles.

One points upward, symbolizing Shiva, the male principle. The other triangle points downward and symbolizes Shakti, the female principle. The star represents the balance that is attained when these two principles are joined in harmony. The star also symbolizes the balancing of energy in the Heart Chakra between the three chakras above it and the three chakras below it. Motivated by love, the desire for sharing, and sympathy, energy can move either downward or upward.

The Circle with Twelve Petals: The star of Anahata Chakra is surrounded by a circle. Twelve deep red (vermilion) lotus petals fold outward from the circle, representing the movement of energy in twelve directions. Energy flows to and from the petals with inhalation and exhalation, activating the twelve mental modifications *(vritties):* (1) hope, (2) anxiety, (3) endeavor, (4) possessiveness, (5) arrogance, (6) incompetence, (7) discrimination, (8) egoism, (9) lustfulness, (10) fraudulence, (11) indecision, and (12) repentance (as stated in the *Mahanirvana Tantra*). The twelve *bija mantras,* which are divinities in sound form, are also seated on these petals.

The Circle with Eight Petals: Inside of the *yantra* there is an additional eight-petaled lotus that is luminous red, like molten gold. It is situated to the right of the physical heart. Its stalk is connected with the goddess Chitrini. In its center a heart is shown that represents the spiritual or etheric heart known as *Ananda Kanda* (Space of Bliss) or *Hrit Pundarik* (Heart Lotus). Stainless and untouched by physical impurities, it is the seat of the Self in waking consciousness and in the dream state. Meditation on this heart is prescribed in many spiritual traditions, as it is supposed to be the temple of God. It can only be reached when the Sushumna starts working.

In the waking state, the physical heart works but the spiritual heart remains dormant. In the dream state, energy from the spiritual heart flows toward the eight petals of the lotus, generating desires and emotional states that are experienced in the waking state. The wakeful desires and emotions change as the energy flows in the direction of different petals, activating the mental modifications *(vritties)* connected with them (see the lotus of the heart diagram).

It is said that there are eight deities, including Indra, on the petals of this lotus. Inside the pericarp is the sun (Vajrini Nadi); inside the sun is the moon (Chitrini Nadi); inside the moon is the fire (Sushumna Nadi). Inside the fire is

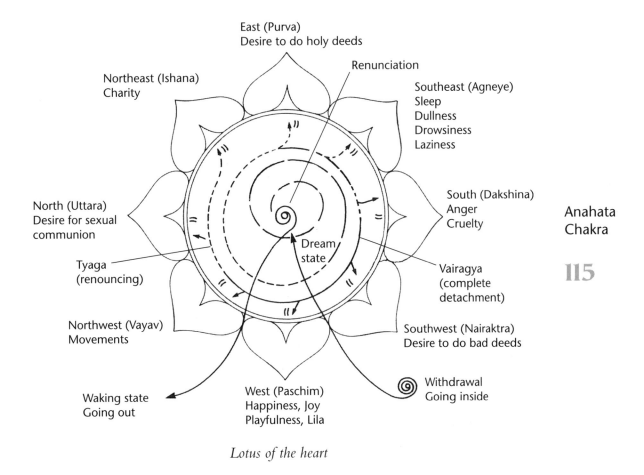

East (Purva)
Desire to do holy deeds

Renunciation

Northeast (Ishana)
Charity

Southeast (Agneye)
Sleep
Dullness
Drowsiness
Laziness

North (Uttara)
Desire for sexual
communion

South (Dakshina)
Anger
Cruelty

Dream
state

Tyaga
(renouncing)

Vairagya
(complete
detachment)

Northwest (Vayav)
Movements

Southwest (Nairaktra)
Desire to do bad deeds

Waking state
Going out

West (Paschim)
Happiness, Joy
Playfulness, Lila

Withdrawal
Going inside

Lotus of the heart

the radiance (Brahma Nadi), where a throne, ornamented with jewels, is located at the base of the wish-fulfilling tree *(kalpa taru)*. On this brightly shining throne is the god Narayana in human form.

Shiva in Bana Lingam: The Bana Lingam radiates with golden light and is formed from a mass of tissues in the nerve center at the Anahata Chakra. Rudra Shiva appears in it as Sada Shiva (*sada* – eternal, *shiva* – benefactor). He is Shabda Brahma, or the eternal Logos. As such he is *Omkara,* the combination of the three *gunas* (qualities) represented by the sounds A, U, and M, which combine to form the sacred syllable AUM or OM. He stands with a trident, also symbolic of the three *gunas: sattva* (equanimity, lightness), *rajas* (mobility, passion), and *tamas* (inertia, darkness). His skin is camphor blue, and he is often shown wearing a golden tiger skin. The drum *(damaru)* that he holds in his other hand maintains the rhythm of the heartbeat.

This *shivalingam,* known as Bana (arrow) Lingam, is the second *lingam* in the chakras. In the first chakra, the Svayambhu Lingam with the Kundalini serpent wrapped around it symbolized the male and female energies, while the *lingam* in this chakra is synonymous with conscience. The force of the Heart Lingam acts as a guru, giving warning or inspiration at each step to guide one along the path of upward energy movement. To heed its guidance, one should keep watch on the heartbeat, for an increase or decrease in the heart rate serves as a warning that there is an error in one's practice.

Element *(Tattva):* Air is colorless and formless, without smell or taste. The *yantra* for air is also described as being gray or smoky green. This information is partly based on scriptural knowledge and partly on information gained by the aspirant during the period of nasal breathing when this element dominates. This takes place soon after the breath changes from one nostril to the other and lasts for eight minutes. Meditation on the fourth chakra brings better results if it is done when the air element dominates and when breath flows through the left nostril, exciting the Ida Nadi.

Seed Sound *(Bija Mantra):* *YANG.* The seed sound of the air element is produced with the tongue resting in the air within the mouth after touching the palate. When this sound is produced properly the spiritual heart vibrates and any blocks in the cardiac region are opened. True knowledge dawns in the consciousness and the second knot, the Vishnu Granthi, is undone, allowing energy to start flowing upward, unobstructed in the Sushumna path. This *bija mantra* gives one control over air, *prana,* and the breath. It aids in the automatic suspension of breath for longer times *(kevali kumbhaka). YANG* is a radiant gold color and is the sound form of the deity Vayu, the lord of the air, who has four arms.

Carrier *(Vahana)* of the Seed Sound: Black antelope or musk deer. The deer or black antelope is the symbol of the heart itself. The antelope is restless, leaps up with joy, and is caught by mirages and reflections. A special quality of the musk deer is that it is enchanted by the smell of musk. Not realizing it is in its own navel, the deer runs everywhere in search of that smell until it gets exhausted. Similarly, the supreme truth, the cosmic consciousness, is in us, yet we are running in search of it in every direction.

Graceful and gentle, the deer depicts the nature of a fourth-chakra person. The eyes of the deer are symbolic of purity and innocence. The eyes of a fourth-chakra person are equally attractive, innocent, and pure. The deer is said to die for pure sound. In the past, hunters would use a flute to play *Todi Raga* to entrap a deer. The love of inner sounds *(anahata nada)* is the love of a fourth-chakra person.

Deity: Ishana Rudra Shiva. The lord of the Northeast, Ishana Shiva is completely detached from the world. He is ever-youthful; the aged, wrathful aspect of Rudra in the third chakra is gone. Ishana is peaceful and beneficent, representing the nature of the fourth-chakra person, which is of perpetual happiness. The holy Ganga (Ganges) flowing from the locks of his hair is a cooling and purifying stream of self-knowledge, the knowledge that "I am That" (*Aham Brahmasmi,* "I am Brahman"). He is camphor blue and wears a tiger skin, symbolic of the tiger of the mind that dwells in the forest of desires. He holds a trident in his right hand and a drum in his left. The snakes coiled around his body are the passions, which he has tamed.

Ishana Rudra Shiva symbolizes that the fourth-chakra person no longer has any attachments to worldly pleasures, honors, or humiliations. Desires have ceased to cause problems, for the energy of the fourth chakra is balanced in all six directions. The person of fourth-chakra awareness lives in harmony with the internal and external worlds.

Shakti: Kakini. The doorkeeper of the Anahata Chakra, Kakini is rose-colored, although the *Mahanirvana Tantra* describes her as being golden yellow or Naples yellow and the *Kankalmalini Tantra* describes her as being white. During different states, her color could change, but meditating on her as rose-colored brings deeper concentration. She has beautiful glittering eyes and is dressed in a light blue sari. Luminous and adorned with golden ornaments, she symbolizes the energy of the fourth chakra, which is self-generating and self-emanating.

Kakini Shakti is all-pervading in the fourth chakra. Like air, she penetrates all places and provides energy to the entire body through the emotional frequencies of devotion *(bhakti)*. In this chakra, *bhakti* is personified as Kundalini Shakti, who aids Kakini Shakti in directing the upward movement of energy.

In her four hands Kakini Shakti holds the implements necessary for attaining balance:

- ꙮ The sword, which provides the means to cut through obstacles blocking the upward flow of energy.

- ꙮ The shield, which protects the aspirant from external worldly conditions.

- ꙮ The skull, which indicates detachment from a false identification with the body.

- ꙮ The trident, which symbolizes the balance of the three forces of preservation, creation, and destruction.

Kakini Shakti has four faces, each of them beautiful like the moon. She is meditated upon as a "moon-faced" *(chandramukhi),* four-headed goddess. Energy flows equally through her four heads into the four aspects of the individual self: the physical self, the rational self, the sensual self, and the emotional self. Kakini is also considered to be the power of Bhuvanesvari, the divine mother, one of the important goddesses of the ten *Mahavidyas.**

Kakini Shakti is auspicious, joyful, and the benefactress of all. She is graceful, confers *siddhis* (powers), and is fully absorbed in concentration. She is the goddess responsible for the creation of devotional poetry, devotional music, and visionary art. Mundane art, poetry, and music, inspired by the Shakti of the second chakra, is unable to elevate the human mind to the higher realms of consciousness, instead serving only to entertain, distract, and stimulate the mind. In contrast, the creativity inspired by Kakini Devi is synchronized with the rhythm of the heart, and thus with the rhythm of the cosmos. It is universal and transcends the limitations of past, present, and future, giving form to the formless, name to the nameless, and audibility to the inaudible. Art, poetry, and music created under the influence of Kakini bring calmness to the mind and peace to the ego and the intellect. At times, this creativity can be so absorbing that the sense of I-consciousness dissolves away.

---

*For further information about the *Mahavidyas* see my book *Tools for Tantra* (Rochester, Vt.: Destiny Books, 1986).

Kundalini Shakti: Kundalini Shakti appears as a beautiful goddess for the first time in the Anahata Chakra. She sits in a lotus posture *(padmasana)* within a triangle. The triangle is pointing upward, showing the tendency of Kundalini Shakti to move upward and carry the aspirant into the higher planes of existence. She is luminous like ten million suns and as cold as ten million moons. Dressed in a white sari, Kundalini Shakti is serene and centered within herself. She is Adya (the first born), Bala Shodashi (the sixteen-year-old virgin), Tripura Sundari (the most beautiful in the three worlds), and Mahavidya or Sri Vidya (spiritual knowledge). She is the personification of selfless spiritual devotion *(bhakti)*, absorbed in meditation on her Lord, and is on her way to union with him. She no longer represents a destructive serpentine force as she did in the first chakra. Instead of being coiled around the *lingam,* she sits independently in a yogic posture. She appears as a young girl, luminous, divine, and enchanting. The aspirant may now communicate with her, gain her favor, and be absorbed in her upward-moving energy, thus crossing the Vishnu Granthi (the emotional knot that attaches one to a certain spiritual order). When the sensory and intellectual mind is completely absorbed in her, divine love pervades the body of the *sadhaka.*

Seated in the lotus posture, Kundalini Shakti embodies *anahata nada,* the cosmic sound that is present everywhere and is known as "white noise." This sound begins in the Heart Chakra as AUM, the seed of all sounds *(shabda brahma).* This sound, called *pranava,* is concentrated *prana* energy, a complex organization of powers in latent form. When the sound potential *(shabda tanmatra)* begins to operate, it manifests as *matrikas* (sound units, letters of the alphabet). It is stated in *Gayatri Tantra* that Kundalini is in the form of fifty *matrikas;* she is Matrika Shakti, the power of speech or sound. She has two forms. One is subtle, beyond sound. In the other, called Mantramayi, she embodies *anahata nada,* all *matrikas,* and all mantras. The sound units arise from her and are embedded in her and finally dissolve in her. Even after the dissolution of the *matrikas,* she remains in her subtle form, which is of the nature of consciousness and is the embodiment of highest spiritual knowledge.

Techniques and Effects of Meditation: The Heart Chakra is revered as a center of devotion and transformation in many spiritual traditions. It shines like a jewel in the center of the spine, the garland of chakras *(chakramala),* with three chakras above and three chakras below. It is mentioned in tantric, puranic, and vedic scriptures under several different names. Sufis and mystics of other traditions instruct their disciples to visualize a clear light in the heart when beginning the practice of raising the Kundalini force and entering higher states of consciousness. It is here that *anahata nada,* or *shabda brahma*—the unstruck cosmic sound— is produced. The spiritual heart of a person is activated by meditation on God (in whatever form one is drawn to) as light enthroned in the spiritual heart at the center of the eight-petaled lotus. That shining light is meditated on as one's true Self. Meditation at this center, aided by *pratyahara* (withdrawal of the senses) and *kumbhaka* (suspension of breath), awakens feelings of renunciation *(sanyasa),* inspiring one to give away all belongings *(tyaga)* and let go of attachments *(vairagya).* It leads to the nondual state of consciousness *(turiya).* It imparts spiritual knowledge and eight super powers *(siddhis)* to the aspirant:

- ∞ *Anima,* atomicity, the power to become very small, almost invisible.

- ∞ *Laghima,* the power to become very light or weightless, the power of levitation.

- ∞ *Mahima,* the power to become big or mighty.

- ∞ *Prapti,* the power to accomplish desires, attainment.

- ∞ *Prakamya,* the power to assume any desired form.

- ∞ *Vashitva,* the power to attract and enslave others by enchantment.

- ∞ *Isthapitva* or *aisvatva,* the power to conquer or subordinate.

- ∞ *Bhukti,* the power to enjoy all kinds of pleasure without indulgence.

Kundalini is aroused through selfless devotion and the dual energy of sound *(matrikas)* and the vital life force *(prana)* in *pranava.* Through the power of *bhakti* (divine love) the devotee achieves a state in which there is only love and the lover, all else vanishes. The plane of sanctity within this chakra brings the perception of the divine (the beloved) in all existence. Roused Kundalini withdraws *prana* slowly and one gradually becomes firm in *asana.* The whole metabolism slows down and a prolonged breath suspension occurs. Feelings are all absorbed in Kundalini. Sensory functions stop and consciousness becomes fully internalized.

A state of refined balance in body and mind is established. Thus, deep concentration starts in the Anahata Chakra. However, Kundalini has yet to cross the Vishuddha Chakra and the Ajna Chakra and pierce the Rudra Granthi (the knot of the attachment to I-consciousness).

By evolving through the fourth chakra, one masters language, poetry and all verbal endeavors. One gains full control of one's work organs and sense organs *(indriyas)*, the mind, desires, and physiological functions. When the senses are controlled, the person flows freely without hindrance from any external barrier. The body becomes free of diseases and attractive to all ages and sexes. Male and female energies become balanced, and the interaction of these two energies outside the body ceases to be a problem, as all relationships become pure. Gaining wisdom and inner strength, the *sadhaka* becomes master *(swami)* of his or her own self. A person centered in the fourth chakra has evolved beyond circumstantial and environmental limitations to become independent and self-emanating. The love and compassion of fourth-chakra persons makes them a source of inspiration to others who find peace and calm in their presence. Fourth-chakra persons worship with love and find love as God everywhere in everything. Faith in themselves and the divine makes them a source of faith for others, even non-believers and atheists. They are harmless and everybody feels secure in their presence.

Behavioral Characteristics of the Anahata Chakra: The Anahata Chakra encompasses *sudharma* (apt or right religion), good tendencies, and the planes of sanctity, balance, and fragrance (the bodies of fourth-chakra persons smell good naturally). However, purgatory may be experienced in the Anahata Chakra when negative karmas are enacted. Clarity of consciousness is the illumination of the pure one who has developed good tendencies and has sanctified his or her life at *Jana Loka,* the human plane, which comes in the fifth chakra.

Fourth-chakra persons have overcome the preoccupations of the lower chakras: security (first chakra), sensuality and sexuality (second chakra), name, fame, authority, social status, power, and physical immortality (third chakra). They have mastered the first five steps of *Ashthanga Yoga (yama, niyama, asana, pranayama,* and *pratyahara),* are centered, and can achieve concentration *(dharana)* to reach meditation *(dhyana).* They will sleep four to six hours nightly, on their left side.

From twenty-one to twenty-eight years of age, one vibrates in the Anahata Chakra, becoming aware of one's role, one's actions, and one's life's goal. Dedication, devotion *(bhakti),* faith, and self-confidence are the motivating forces as one strives to achieve balance at all levels. Following a spiritual path makes it easy for a fourth-chakra person to realize the truth beyond words. Surrender to a guru or dedicating one's life to a cause such as that of removing suffering or ignorance helps one to restrain oneself from running after mirages like an antelope, being restless, wandering, and purposeless.

A spiritually inspired fourth-chakra person is a saint or saintly person. (A saint belongs to a particular order, but a saintly person does not need initiation to behave with love and compassion). Such a person is free from anger, lust, jealousy, and other mental modifications *(vritties).* He or she is friendly, loving, patient, calm, and has an influence on others that helps them get away from all worries and anxieties. The movement of fourth-chakra persons is rhythmic and graceful and love can be seen flowing constantly through their eyes, touch, hand gestures—their whole person. They are both childlike and wise, respectful and respected by all.

If the heart has been opened, it is possible for a person who is not spiritually inclined to be good—a good father, mother, brother, sister, husband, or wife. Selfless service creates such fourth-chakra persons who do not follow any spiritual path but are friendly and loving to all. They may not even believe in God in a traditional sense but are spiritual and saintly. They enjoy everything as it is presented, without thinking about what it should be or what it could be; their unconditional enjoyment of each moment opens the way to the fourth chakra. If the feeling of motherhood is awakened in a person, that automatically helps to open the heart or increase the flow of energy in the fourth chakra, making the behavior of such a person very soothing to others.

VISHUDDHA CHAKRA
(FIFTH CHAKRA)

Names:	Vishuddha, Kanth Padma, Shodash Dala
Meanings of the Names:	Pure, Throat Lotus (*kanth* - throat, *padma* - lotus), Sixteen-petaled (*shodash* - sixteen, *dala* - petals)
Location:	Neck region, throat; carotid plexus, the cervical part of the spinal column that corresponds to the neck
Element *(Tattva):*	*Akasha*
Color of the Element:	Smoky purple
Shape *(Yantra)* of the Element:	Crescent
Seed Sound *(Bija Mantra)* of the Element:	*HANG*
Color of the Seed Sound:	Gold
Carrier *(Vahana)* of the Seed Sound:	Elephant *(gaja)*
Number of Petals:	Sixteen
Color of the Petals:	Lavender gray, smoky purple
Seed Sounds of the Petals:	ANG, ĀNG, ING, ĪNG, UNG, ŪNG, ṚING, ṚĪNG, ḶRING, ḶRĪNG, ENG, AING, ONG, AUNG, ANG, AHANG
Aspects:	Knowledge
Predominant Sense:	Hearing
Sense Organ:	Ears
Work Organ:	Mouth, vocal cords
Air *(Vayu, Prana):*	*Udana,* the air that dwells in the throat and head region that carries air up through the head, aiding in the production of sound
Plane *(Loka):*	Human plane *(Jana Loka)* where the great spiritual darkness ends
Ruling Planet:	Jupiter

Yantra **Form:** The crescent, with a white circle inside of it. The circle represents the *nabhomandala* (*nabha* – sky or void, *mandala* – region). It is like a full moon shining in the pericarp of the Vishuddha Chakra. The silver crescent is the lunar

123

Vishuddha Chakra

विशुद्ध चक्र

Bija petal sound

अं आं इं ईं उं ऊं ऋं ॠं ऌं ॡं एं ऐं ओं औं अं अः

symbol of *nada,* pure cosmic sound. Thus the void *(akasha)* is inside of the pure essence *(tanmatra)* of sound *(nada)*. The crescent is a symbol of purity and *akasha* is the purest of all the elements. Purification is a vital aspect of the Vishuddha Chakra, as is pure knowledge *(shuddha vidya)*, known in Tantra as the ten *Mahavidyas* or *Sri Vidya.*

The moon in any of its aspects implies psychic energy, clairvoyance, and communication without words. The moon also depicts the presence of a cooling mechanism in the throat by which all liquids and foods are brought to a temperature suited to the body.

The Circle with Sixteen Petals: The sixteen lotus petals around the crescent and circle are lavender gray or smoky purple. There are sixteen vowels *(matrikas)* on the petals, each of which combines with NG to make a seed sound (e.g., *A + NG = ANG, I + NG = ING). NG* is *nada-bindu,* the primal cosmic sound from which the universe manifested, represented by the crescent *(nada)* and dot *(bindu)* above it.

There are sixteen specific qualities *(vritties)* on the sixteen petals of the Vishuddha Chakra. Most of them are connected to musical sound, frequencies in a harmonic scale, and mantras used for the invocation of divinities within the body. They are arranged from the right to left in the following order: (1) *pranava,* the mantra *AUM,* pronounced as *Ong;* (2) *udgitha,* the mantra from *Sama Veda* in seed form; then six mantras: (3) *HANG,* (4) *PHAT,* (5) *VASHAT,* (6) *SWADHA,* (7) *SWAHA,* and (8) *NAMAH;* (9) *amrita* (immortality); and seven musical tones: (10) *Nishad,* (11) *Rishabha,* (12) *Gandhar,* (13) *Shadja,* (14) *Madhyam,* (15) *Dhaivat,* and (16) *Pancham.* The musical tones are not in the same order as in a musical scale. *HANG, PHAT, VASHAT,* and *SWADHA* are mantras used in all Tantric practices. *SWAHA* is used in a fire ceremony *(homa). NAMAH* is used to pay respect. They all belong to deities or divinities that rule the petals and provide energy to the qualities *(vritties)*. The increase in the number of petals around the *yantra* comes to an end at this chakra.

Element *(Tattva)*: *Akasha.* At the Vishuddha Chakra, the aspirant gets a vision of the void *(akasha),* which is of the nature of anti-matter. *Akasha* is also the holder of all existence and is thus also translated as space. *Akasha* is generated by the principle *(tanmatra)* of sound. There are five different kinds of *akasha:*

ଙ *Abhrakasha,* the atmospheric void.

ଙ *Jalakasha,* the void in water.

ଙ *Ghatakasha,* the void in an empty vessel or water pot.

ଙ *Patakasha,* the void in relation to a surface. It is related with the *akasha* created by *mantra japa* (mantra repetition), called *mastak patal,* which includes the void created by inaudible sound frequencies *(nada).* It is also related to the emotional state produced by the experience of listening to music in the heart that continues even after the audible sound frequencies stop *(hridaya patal).*

ଙ *Mahakasha,* the supreme void in which only nothingness *(shunya)* exists. According to Buddha, this void *(shunya)* is the ultimate reality.

Meditation on the Vishuddha Chakra brings the best results when it is done in the presence of the *akasha* element, which dominates for four minutes when breath flows through either of the two nostrils, just before the breathing changes from one nostril to the other. This meditation opens the Sushumna passage and activates the Sushumna Nadi. Normally the Sushumna is activated only during the ten breaths per hour when breathing from both nostrils occurs simultaneously, but it is possible to prolong its activity. The operation of the Sushumna stops the flow of energy through the Ida and Pingala Nadis, thus releasing the aspirant from time-bound consciousness.

In the Vishuddha Chakra all the elements of the lower chakras are refined to their purest essence and dissolved in *akasha,* depicted by the circle and crescent at the top of the temple *(stupa)* within the body (see diagram). The influence of the elements *(mahabhutas* or *tattvas)* ceases after the fifth chakra and the aspirant becomes a *tattvatit,* one who has gone beyond the grip of the elements.

Seed Sound (Bija Mantra): *HANG.* The sound *HANG* is produced by forming an oval shape with the lips and pushing the air outward from the throat. Concentration is centered in the hollow curve of the lower neck. When this sound is produced properly, it vibrates the brain and causes the cerebrospinal fluid to flow more freely into the throat region, bringing sweet and melodious qualities to the voice. The color of the *bija mantra HANG* is gold, although it is also described as being of radiant white color with four arms.

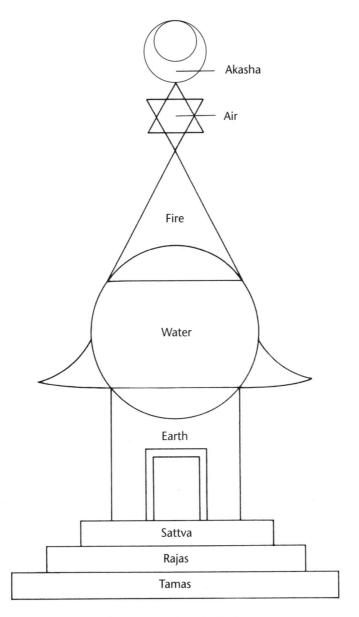

Akasha

Air

Fire

Water

Earth

Sattva

Rajas

Tamas

The stupa within the body

Carrier *(Vahana)* of the Seed Sound: The elephant *(gaja),* the lord of herbivorous animals. The most primitive of surviving mammals, it carries the entire past knowledge of earth, herbs, and plants. The elephant is considered to be one who teaches patience, memory, self-confidence, and the enjoyment of synchronicity with nature. It is smoky gray in color, the color of the clouds, although it is sometimes shown as a snow elephant of white color. The confidence and consciousness about sound that come in the Vishuddha Chakra are indicated by the graceful gait and large ears of the elephant.

The single trunk represents pure sound. As mentioned above, the addition of the *NG* sound to the letters of the alphabet *(matrikas)* turns them into *bija mantras*. The *NG* sounds are nasal, like the elephant's sound, *Nishad* or *Ni* (one of the notes of the musical scale), which is produced by its trunk rather than its vocal chords. The nasal sounds move energy upward to vibrate the outermost brain cortex where impressions are stored, which, when converted into language, carry the wisdom and knowledge that bring liberation from the cycle of birth and death.

Deity: Panchavaktra Shiva. Panchavaktra is a combination of all the *shiva*-energies, which work in different directions and in the different elements. His five heads represent the five *tanmatras* (principles) as well as the five elements that evolve from them: earth from *gandha* (smell), water from *rasa* (taste), fire from *rupa* (sight), air from *sparsha* (touch), and *akasha* from *shabda* (sound). Here they are united in one body. Beginning with his right side, the faces of Shiva symbolize his aspects as follows :

- ೞ Aghora, the lord of the North. He is wide-eyed in his wrathful form and resides in the cremation ground. Aghora is beyond discrimination. His face is rounded and his nature is that of *akasha*.

- ೞ Ishana, the lord of the Northeast. He appears in shrines as a *shivalingam*. His face is round and his nature is that of water.

- ೞ Tat Purusha, the lord of the East. His oval face is the central one of the five. His nature is that of air. Tat Purusha is Mahadeva. He is always seen in meditation, where he has controlled *prana* and achieved *kevala kumbhaka* (automatic breath suspension).

- ೞ Vama Deva, the eternal Shiva who expands in all directions. He has a square face and his nature is that of earth. Vama Deva is Sada Shiva, represented as the lord or giver of left-handed Tantra *(bhoga* for *yoga)*.

- ೞ Saddyojat, the lord of the South. His face is triangular and his nature is that of fire. Saddyojat is Rudra, the wrathful deity in the third chakra. He is shown as Braddha Rudra (Old Shiva), but usually he is portrayed as the awesome youthful Shiva.

Panchavaktra is shown with four arms. His upper right hand is in a gesture of *abhai mudra,* granting fearlessness. In his lower right hand, resting on his knee, he holds a *mala* (rosary) for *japa* (mantra repetition). His lower left hand holds a *damaru* which drones continuously, producing the fourteen sounds known as *Maheshvara Sutras,* from which all the vowels and consonants of the Sanskrit language evolve. The continuous sound of the drum also creates the sound *AUM* in its overtones. His upper left hand holds a trident, the staff of Shiva, which symbolizes the three *gunas (sattva, rajas,* and *tamas)* and the three Nadis (Ida, Pingala, and Sushumna).

Panchavaktra may be visualized in the fifth chakra as the Great Teacher or Master Guru. In him, all the elements have dissolved into one. The fifth-chakra person thus understands the limitations of each element and the human plane in its totality. The awareness of eternal knowledge is grasped when all desires move upward into the sixth chakra. Centering by balancing all of the bodily elements brings a state of blissful non-duality. Through meditation on Panchavaktra, one is elevated and cleansed from all karmas; one dies to the past and is born again into the realization of oneness.

Shakti: Shakini. The doorkeeper of the Vishuddha Chakra, Shakini is an embodiment of purity. She is splendorous, delightful, and peace giving. Her five heads indicate the five senses connected with the lower five chakras and their respective elements. Her skin is pale rose and she wears a sky blue sari with a green bodice. However, some sources describe her as being white, with yellow raiment, while others describe her as being red, with black raiment. We meditate on her as pale rose, with sky blue raiment, sitting in the lotus posture *(padmasana)* on a pink lotus.

Shakini Shakti is the bestower of higher knowledge and *siddhis* (powers). Memory, ready wit, intuition, and improvisation are all related to Shakini Shakti. The fifth chakra is the center of dreams in the body and most of the teachings of Shakini Shakti are revealed to her aspirants through dreams. Her four arms hold the following objects:

ଔ A skull, which is a symbol of detachment from the illusory world of sense perceptions.

- An *ankusha,* a staff used to control the elephant of intellect, which can be overly independent, moving in its own intoxication of knowledge.

  The scriptures, representing knowledge of the art of right living without complexes.

- A rosary *(mala),* which acts as a powerful centering device when used as an accompaniment to mantra repetition. The beads are touched by the fingers, one by one. When the beads are made of wood or seeds, they absorb and retain the person's own energy. When the beads are cut from crystals, gems, or other precious materials, they are highly charged with their own electromagnetic energy. The fingertips are directly related to consciousness, so engagement of the fingertips is the engagement of consciousness. Working with the *mala* thus removes nervousness and distractions, and pacifies the internal dialogue.

Techniques and Effects of Meditation: Meditation on the Vishuddha Chakra is centered on the hollow space in the throat region that represents the element *akasha.* After the energy has stopped flowing in the Ida and Pingala Nadis, *akasha* is experienced as the void *(shunya)* during the operation of the Sushumna. However, this meditation is still affected by the three *gunas: sattva* (equanimity, lightness), *rajas* (mobility, passion), and *tamas* (inertia, darkness). Their influence does not cease completely until the aspirant crosses the Ajna Chakra, where *akasha* also merges in Kundalini Shakti.

Spoken words come from the fifth chakra, giving expression to the emotions within the heart. The voice of a fifth-chakra person penetrates to the heart of the listener. This pure sound affects the listener by changing the space *(akasha)* of his or her mind and being. Prayers and devotional songs *(bhajans)* arise from the heart (Anahata Chakra) and are expressed by the vocal chords in the throat, while mantras arise from the Vishuddha Chakra itself and are expressed by the throat. Thus, songs create a spiritual state, which is trance-like, but mantras bring out divine energies and give form to the formless.

Meditation on the Vishuddha Chakra gives calmness, serenity, purity, a melodious voice, the command of speech and mantras, and the ability to compose poetry. It makes one youthful, radiant (full of *ojas*), and capable of understanding the hidden messages in dreams. It confers the power of interpreting scriptures and of being a good teacher of spiritual sciences *(Brahma Vidya, Shuddha Vidya, Sri Vidya)*. Meditation on *akasha* also gives one the ability to travel through space and other *siddhis*.

Behavioral Characteristics in the Vishuddha Chakra: The Vishuddha Chakra is the chakra of spiritual rebirth. It encompasses the five planes: physical, astral, celestial, balance, and human. It also includes *jnana,* awareness that bestows bliss; *prana,* the vital life force throughout the body that brings balance of all the elements; *apana,* the air that cleanses the body and is charged with negative ions; and *vyana,* the air that regulates the blood flow. The human plane *(jana loka)* becomes vital, enriched with mantras, musical sounds, and the sixteen harmonious qualities *(vritties)*.

Behavior is well defined in the lower chakras, but there are no distinct worldly characteristics in the fifth chakra, as it is only reached by spiritual teachers. Vishnu Granthi, which usually stops the flow of energy above the fourth chakra, can only be unknotted by true spiritual knowledge. Aspirants who practice Kundalini Yoga of any form reach this chakra, and their behavior is simple living and high thinking. They spend more time inside than outside. They sleep between four to six hours nightly, changing sides.

The qualities *(vritties)* in this chakra do not create distractions, but lead the aspirant to the sciences of mantras and harmonic sound frequencies, which absorb the mind and let the energy move upward to undo the last knot, the knot of I-consciousness, Rudra Granthi. The fifth chakra person comprehends non-verbal messages, for all energy has been refined.

Persons between the ages of twenty-eight and thirty-five are influenced by the Vishuddha Chakra. I-consciousness and spiritual growth motivate the fifth-chakra person. The fifth-chakra aspirant seeks knowledge that is true, beyond the limitations of time, cultural conditioning, and genetic code. The main problem encountered in the fifth chakra is doubt or negative intellect. When knowledge is used unwisely, doubt comes, but when the aspirant trusts only what he or she can verify through meditation and experience, doubts are removed and negativity dissolves. Consciousness is still time-bound, but the disciplines of Ashtanga Yoga bring self-mastery and freedom from the fetters of worldliness.

The Vishuddha Chakra is ruled by the planet Jupiter, which makes fifth-chakra persons interested in scriptures of ancient knowledge. Jupiter is called "guru" in Sanskrit, which means "dispeller of darkness." The writings of fifth-chakra persons are like scriptures, revealing and illuminating. Their very presence removes ignorance by opening up channels of knowledge within their listeners, enabling them to receive illumination and be freed from darkness. An aura can be seen around the head of a fifth-chakra person. Just as all elements dissolve in pure and self-luminous *akasha,* all worldliness dissolves in the presence of such a person, because the distractions created by the senses and mind cease to be a problem.

AJNA CHAKRA
(SIXTH CHAKRA)

Names:	Ajna, Bhru Madhya, Dvidal Padma
Meanings of the Names:	Command, Point Between the Eyebrows (*bhru* - eyebrows, *madhya* - in between), Two-petaled Lotus (*dvi* - two, *dal* - petal, *padma* - lotus)
Location:	Medulla plexus, pineal plexus, point between the eyebrows
Element *(Tattva)*:	*Mahat* or *mahatattva* (supreme or great element) in which all other elements are present in their pure essence
Color of the Element:	Transparent, luminescent, bluish or camphor white
Shape *(Yantra)* of the Element:	A circle with two petals
Seed Sound *(Bija Mantra)* of the Element:	*AUM*
Color of the Seed Sound:	Gold
Carrier *(Vahana)* of the Seed Sound:	Nada in the form of a crescent
Seed Sounds of the Petals:	*HANG, KSHANG*
Aspects:	Self-realization
Plane *(Loka)*:	Plane of austerity or penance (*Tapas Loka*)
Ruling Planet:	Saturn

Yantra **Form:** Luminescent white circle with two petals. These petals are the habenulae of the pineal gland. Meditation on the seed sounds of the petals *(HANG, KSHANG)* activates the *matrikas* that are connected with the three Nadis of Vama, Jyeshtha, and Raudri.

Lingam: A *lingam* known as the Itara Lingam appears in the center of the circle. It has the seed sound *AUM* and is luminescent white with a little touch of cerulean blue. The third *lingam* of the chakras, it represents Itara Shiva, who has the power of full control over desires, because he controls the subtle mind (*sukshma manas*). The subtle mind is beyond the operation of the senses, which are situated in the lower five chakras.

133

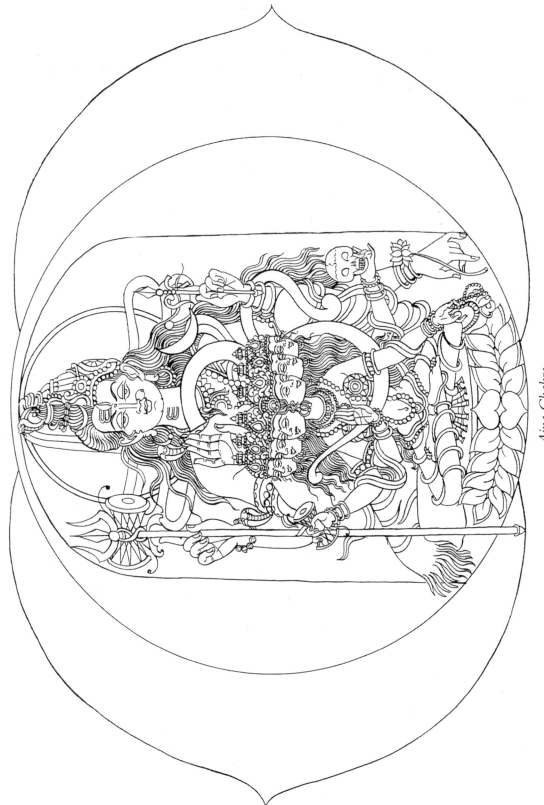

Ajna Chakra

आज्ञा चक्र

Bija petal sound

हंक्ष

Seed Sound *(Bija Mantra)* of the Element: *AUM.* The pranava, *AUM,* is the source of all sounds and is connected with the *anahata nada,* the primal cosmic sound. It thus creates unity and nondual consciousness. It is a combination of sun *(A),* moon *(U),* and fire *(M).*

Carrier *(Vahana)* of the Seed Sound: *AUM* is carried by *nada,* which is represented by a crescent moon. It is also known as *ardhamatra (ardha* - half, *matra* - alphabet).

Element: *Mahat* or *Mahatattva.* According to Samkhya philosophy, *mahatattva* consists of the three *gunas* and includes mind *(manas),* intellect *(buddhi),* I-consciousness *(ahamkara),* being *(chitta),* and the five basic principles *(tanmatras).* The gross elements *(mahabhutas)*—earth, air, fire, water, and *akasha*—evolve from

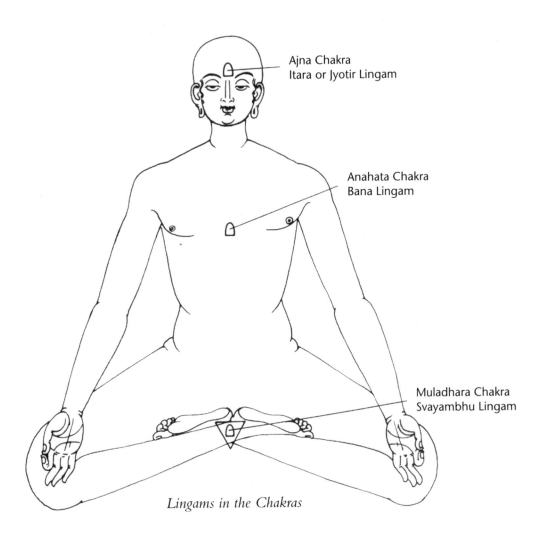

Ajna Chakra
Itara or Jyotir Lingam

Anahata Chakra
Bana Lingam

Muladhara Chakra
Svayambhu Lingam

Lingams in the Chakras

mahatattva. According to Tantra, *mahatattva* is *buddhi tattva*, the cause of *manas*, *buddhi*, *ahamkara*, and *chitta*.

Deity: Ardhanarishvara (*ardha* - half, *nari* - female, *Ishvara* - Shiva) stands or is seated gracefully inside the *lingam*. The half-male, half-female Shiva-Shakti is symbolic of basic polarity: the right side is male, solar, and the left side is female, lunar. Ardhanarishvara is camphor blue on the Shiva side and pale pink on the Shakti side.

The two right hands belong to Shiva. In one he holds a trident, representing the three aspects of consciousness—cognition, conation, and affection. With his other hand he grants fearlessness. The left hands belong to Shakti. In one she holds a lotus, a symbol of beauty, purity, and knowledge (which keeps one untouched by one's surroundings). In her other hand she holds a staff used to control an elephant *(ankusha)*. Shiva wears a tiger skin, which symbolizes control over the animal nature of the mind, and is decorated with snakes, symbolizing control of the poison of the passions. Shakti wears a red sari and blouse and is decorated with golden ornaments.

Ardhanarishvara symbolizes that all duality has ceased. There is only one entity, self-emanating and illustrious, which has complete command over all aspects of the Self in this plane of liberation *(moksha)*. The third eye of Shiva is called *sva netra* (*sva* - own, *netra* - eye). It is the eye of the I-consciousness, the organ of clairvoyance, the eye that sees all three divisions of time—past, present, and future *(trikal darshi)*. The two eyes are related with the Ida and the Pingala, and the third eye is in the Sushumna, in the Chitrini Nadi. When the two external eyes close, the internal third eye opens up and consumes the source of desires *(kama)* in its fire.

Shakti: Hakini. Goddess Hakini is the doorkeeper of the sixth chakra. Through concentration on her the *sadhaka* gets all the necessary powers and qualities to be able to work in the Ajna Chakra. The pale pink color of her body indicates the fully aroused Kundalini, absorbing all energies and moving upwards. Like the Shaktis in the lower five chakras, Hakini is an aspect of Kundalini Shakti. Kundalini has gained an additional head with each chakra so that here she has six heads, which indicate: (1) enlightenment, (2) thought control, (3) undivided attention, (4) perfect concentration, (5) unobstructed meditation, and (6) super-conscious concentration *(samprajnata samadhi)*.

She is seated on a light pink lotus and has four hands. In her upper right hand is the drum *(damaru),* which maintains a steady drone and leads the aspirant to higher states of consciousness. *Damaru* here signifies *nada.* Her lower right hand is in *abhai mudra,* the gesture of bestowing fearlessness. In her upper left hand she holds a skull, a symbol of total detachment. Her lower left hand holds a rosary *(mala),* for use with mantra repetition as a centering device.

It is said that an aspirant will experience the presence of *soma* (nectar) when he or she meditates on Hakini. Soma comes from the Kamadhenu, the wish-fulfilling cow, who is in the Soma Chakra. If the yogi practices *khechari mudra* (explained on pages 62–63 in chapter 2, "Kundalini and Yoga"), he or she absorbs this nectar of immortality instead of allowing it to reach the throat, thus gaining the power to remain youthful.

Techniques and Effects of Meditation: Ajna Chakra is the place of meditation. Many Hindus wear a vermilion or saffron colored mark on this spot between the eyebrows to activate their third eye, which is the conscience. The two physical eyes see the past and the present, while the third eye reveals the future. All experiences and ideas serve only to clarify one's perceptions in Ajna Chakra.

The two physical eyes represent the sun and moon, and the third eye, the fire. These are the three basic principles of manifested consciousness. In the sixth chakra, the Ida and Pingala Nadis terminate in their respective nostrils. The three "rivers" of Ida (lunar current), Pingala (solar current), and Sushumna (central, neutral current) meet in Triveni, the main seat of consciousness. After crossing the fifth chakra and before reaching Ajna Chakra, the Sushumna bifurcates. The anterior branch continues upward with the Vajrini, Chitrini, Vama, Jyeshtha, Raudri, and Brahma Nadis, while the posterior branch has only the fire element. The sun works as the Pingala Nadi outside the Sushumna and as the Vajrini and Jyeshtha Nadis inside. The moon works as the Ida Nadi outside the Sushumna and as the Chitrini and Vama Nadis inside. The fire works as the posterior Sushumna and, inside the anterior Sushumna, as the Raudri Nadi and the Brahma Nadi, the innermost Nadis.

The posterior Sushumna consumes in its fire all the impressions *(samskaras)* that are stored in the *buddhi* (intellect). Concentration on the seed sound *AUM,* especially on the *bindu* (the dot above the crescent in the syllable *AUM* written in

Sanskrit script), is helpful in activating the flow of energy through the posterior Sushumna. The third eye (pineal) plays an important role in the piercing or unknotting of the third knot, Rudra Granthi, which is in the path of the anterior Sushumna. I-consciousness is destroyed by meditating on the Goddess Hakini's first four heads, indicating enlightenment, thought control, undivided attention, and perfect concentration. In real meditation neither the meditator *(dhyata)* nor the one who is meditated upon *(dhaiye)* exist. However, meditation on a particular aspect of divinity focuses the mind, enhancing the aspirant's ability to maintain concentration. Ultimately, concentration on the *lingam* provides the power to absorb thoughts and transform concentration into meditation. The reduction of the *lingam* to the *bindu* is the process of absorptive concentration.

When the yogi performs *mantra japa* (sound repetition) on *SOHAM*, "That I am" *(sa* - that, *aham* - I am) in the sixth chakra, the syllables automatically become reversed, forming the mantra *HAMSA,* which is the Sanskrit word for swan, the bird that can fly to places unknown to ordinary people. Thus, meditation on the Self *(atman)* in the *bindu* (the dot representing infinity in the syllable *AUM),* transforms the yogi into a *paramahamsa,* one who dwells in supreme consciousness.

Those who meditate on this chakra eradicate all of their sins or impurities and enter the seventh door, beyond Ajna Chakra. The aura of such persons enables all who come into their presence to become calm and sensitive to the refined sound frequencies of *AUM;* the *AUM* drone generates from their body itself. They are now *tattvatita,* beyond the *tattvas* (elements). All desires are basically the play of *tattva.* Those who have established themselves in the place between the eyebrows go beyond all the kinds of desires that motivate life and prompt movement in many directions. They become one-pointed. Because they have brought the breath and the mind under control, they maintain a continual state of *samadhi* (realized nonduality) during all actions. Whatever they desire comes true.

Behavioral Characteristics in the Ajna Chakra: This chakra encompasses the solar *(Yamuna),* lunar *(Ganga),* earthly *(Prithvi),* and liquid *(Jala)* planes, and the planes of conscience *(Viveka),* neutrality *(Sarasvati),* austerity *(Tapas),* violence *(Himsa),* and spiritual devotion *(Bhakti).* The solar and lunar nerve energies intertwine up through all chakras and join into one at the sixth chakra. The plane of neutrality appears as a balance between solar and lunar energy within the body. The components of duality become equalized, leaving a state of pure music and neutrality. This brings the sense of oneness and of unity with the cosmic laws that appear in the plane of austerity. The person realizes that he or she is the immortal spirit in a temporal body. The liquid plane cools any excessive heat generated by increased powers and purifies the conscience. The plane of spiritual devotion maintains proper balance within the yogi.

The Ajna Chakra is associated with the pineal gland, which protrudes into the third ventricle and is surrounded by cerebrospinal fluid. The pineal helps to regulate the flow of this clear watery fluid from the Soma Chakra, which lies above the Ajna, through the ventricles of the brain, and downward through the spinal cord to the base of the spine. The pineal itself responds very sensitively to light. When a person enters Ajna Chakra, light will form around his or her head and aura.

The Ida and the Pingala Nadis are time-bound, so up to the fifth chakra the yogi also is time-bound, but as the Ida and the Pingala end in the sixth chakra, the yogi moves into the Sushumna, which is beyond time *(kalatita)*. He or she becomes a knower of the past, present, and future *(trikaladarshi)*. For sixth-chakra persons, the danger of backsliding ends; there is no spiritual reversal. For as long as they are in their physical body, they are in a constant state of nondual consciousness. They can enter any other body at will. They are able to comprehend the inner meaning of cosmic knowledge and are able to generate scriptures.

In the Ajna Chakra the yogi becomes a divine manifestation, embodying all of the elements in their purest form or essence. All external and internal changes cease to pose problems. The mind reaches a state of undifferentiated cosmic awareness. All duality ceases. The person evolved through the Ajna Chakra reveals the divine within and reflects divinity within others. In the fourth chakra one evolves through *ananda* (beatitude), and in the fifth, through *chit* (cosmic consciousness). In the sixth, one becomes *sat* (true). There is no observed and no observer. One attains the realization "That I am; I am That," and thus embodies *sat-chit-ananda,* or "being-consciousness-bliss."

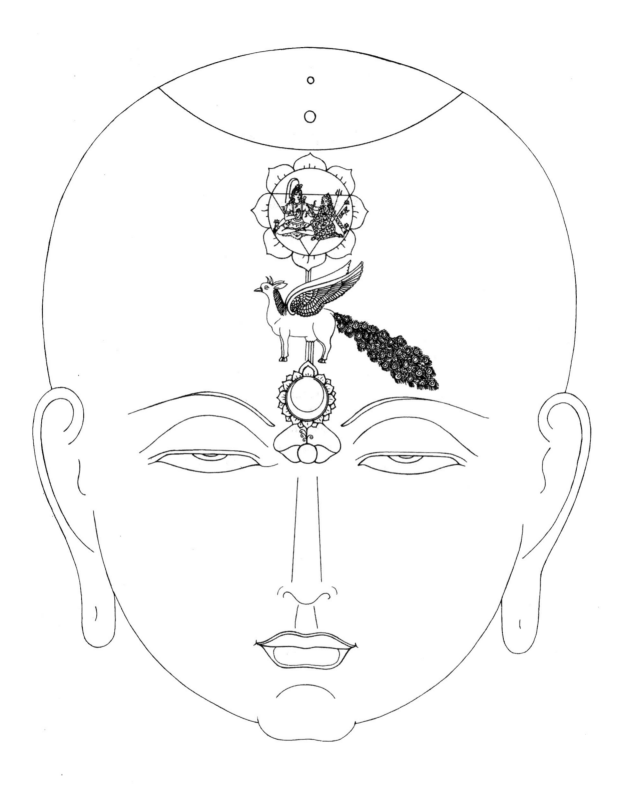

Soma Chakra

सोम चक्र

SOMA CHAKRA

Names:	Soma, Amrita, Indu
Meanings of the Names:	Nectar or Moon,
	Nectar of Immortality, Moon
Location:	Above the Ajna Chakra and
	within the Sahasrara or seventh
	Chakra, above the third eye in
	the center of the forehead
Ruling Planet:	Rahu

Yantra **Form:** Crescent of silver color in a lotus of light blue white. Sometimes the crescent is also colored white to indicate the domination of *sattva* in this chakra. The lotus has twelve petals, although some scriptures indicate sixteen petals. The crescent moon in the center of the lotus is the source of nectar *(soma)* for the body. However, it receives nectar from Kamadhenu, the wish-fulfilling cow, and three of the Nadis: Ambika, Lambika, and Talika. The nectar is constantly seeping out of the *nirjhar gupha,* or *brahmar gupha,* "the cave of the bumble bee," the hollow space between the twin hemispheres of the brain.

Kamadhenu: The color of Kamadhenu is white. She has the face of a crow, which stands for alertness; the horns of a cow, which symbolizes nourishment; the neck of a horse, which symbolizes strength; the tail of a peacock, which is associated with fantasies and dreams; and the wings of a white swan *(hamsa),* which stands for the quality of discrimination. Her forehead is *ahamkara* (the ego), and her eyes are human, of pure nature. This wish-fulfilling cow becomes accessible to the yogi when he or she has pierced through the Rudra Granthi and the I-consciousness has dissolved. The yogi's wishes are then universal needs, and they are fulfilled by concentration on Kamadhenu.

Kameshvara Chakra: The Kameshvara Chakra is located just above the spot where Kamadhenu resides. Although it is another minor chakra within the Sahasrara Chakra, it is a chakra of utmost importance. It is here that the goddess Kundalini, in the form of Kameshvari, is united with her lord, Param Shiva, in

141

the form of Kameshvara. In tantric practice, Kundalini is awakened and aroused to seek this union with Shiva, the summum bonum of Kundalini Yoga. Kundalini (the spiritual consciousness of the individual) no longer has any separate existence; she is completely absorbed into Param Shiva (the supreme consciousness).

Ā-KĀ-THĀ Triangle: Within the Kameshvara Chakra is a triangle surrounding Kameshvari and Kameshvara. Known in Tantra Yoga as the Ā-KĀ-THĀ Triangle, it is formed by the three Nadis of Vama, Jyeshtha, and Raudri. In the Muladhara Chakra the same three Nadis form a triangle that surrounds Shiva and Shakti (in the form of the Svayambhu Lingam with Kundalini coiled around it). Prior to manifestation, *param bindu* (supreme consciousness) assumes a three-fold character represented as the three specific power points *(bindus)* of the triangles. Together, the three *bindus*—*rakta* (red) *bindu, shvait* (white) *bindu,* and mixed colors *bindu*—are *kamkala,* the principle of the actualization of energized consciousness (Shakti) as subtle sound frequencies. They represent three kinds of forces *(bindus): bindu, bija,* and *nada.* They are also known as: Brahmi, the energy of Brahma, the creator; Vaishnavi, the energy of Vishnu, the preserver; and Maheshvari, the energy of Maheshvara, the destroyer, who is the lord of lords, Shiva himself. These three Shaktis flow through the three Nadis of Vama, Jyeshtha, and Raudri, respectively, and represent the three aspects of consciousness:knowing, feeling, and doing. When Kundalini is aroused to flow upward by the constant practice of *pranayama, mantra japa,* and concentration, all aspects of the individual and the manifested world are absorbed in Kundalini Shakti. When she unites with the supreme consciousness in Kameshvara Chakra, the three gunas *(sattva, rajas, and tamas)* also merge and the energy of the three *bindus* is reabsorbed into the supreme *bindu.* Truth *(satyam),* beauty *(sundaram),* and goodness *(shivam)*—which emanate from knowing, feeling, and doing—are realized in all forms of expression and incorporated into one's behavior. Thus the highest aim of life is achieved.

Deities: Kameshvara and Kameshvari. Kameshvara is Lord Shiva himself. He is the lord of the desire principle (*kama* - desire, *ishvara* - lord). He is the one whom Kameshvari, the goddess of desire, is eager to meet. Once she is aroused, she rushes to meet her lord through the narrow passage of Brahma Nadi, using any of the five movements (described on pages 68–69 in chapter 2, "Kundalini and Yoga"). Turning up the petals of all the lotuses of the different chakras, she

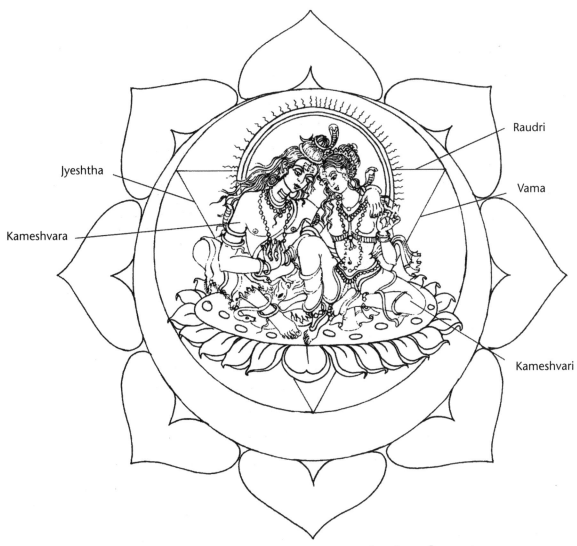

Jyeshtha

Kameshvara

Raudri

Vama

Kameshvari

Kameshvara and Kameshvari seated in the Ā-KĀ-THĀ Triangle

ASPECTS OF CONSCIOUSNESS					
Vama	Volition (Iccha)	Feeling	Subtle Sound (Pashyanti)	Creation	Brahmi
Jyeshtha	Knowledge (Jnana)	Knowing	Intermediate Sound (Madhyama)	Preservation	Vaishnavi
Raudri	Action (Kriya)	Doing	Articulated Sound (Vaikhari)	Dissolution	Maheshvari

reaches the highest chakra to meet him. Kameshvara is described as the most beautiful of male forms. He is seated like a yogi, but in eternal embrace with his beloved Kameshvari, who is the most beautiful female in the three worlds, Tripura Sundari (*tri* - three, *pura* - planes or worlds, *sundari* - beautiful).

Kameshvara is also known as Urdhvareta (*urdhva* -upward, *reta* - streaming or flowing), for his ability to draw the essence of the seminal fluid upward through the Sushumna Nadi; he is lord of the knowledge of the upward movement of energy. Vamachara (left-handed) Tantra provides a complete description of this process of upward movement and claims that the physical male seed *(bindu)* must be brought to the Kameshvara Chakra to unite with the lunar female energy. The interior and exterior union becomes *tantra* (expanded consciousness), because it is a combination of *bhoga* (enjoyment) and *yoga* (detachment). Kameshvara bestows the power of upward movement and the retention of seed; therefore meditation on Kameshvara causes the ego to subside, and the yogi sitting in Soma Chakra enjoys *brahmananda* (the bliss of *brahman*). Kameshvari is no longer the furious serpent (Kundalini) who breathes out fire, as she was when suddenly awakened from her sleep. Kameshvari, the desiring one, is now at peace, in union with her beloved, Kameshvara, the one who fulfills all desires.

Techniques and Effects of Meditation: In its natural course, *soma* (nectar) flows downward from Kamadhenu through the chakras. When it reaches the Manipura Chakra, the third chakra, it is burned by the fire energy of the solar plexus. However, yogis can block the downward flow of this nectar *(amrita)* by meditating on the eight-petaled lotus of Kameshvara Chakra and performing *khechari mudra* (described on pages 62–63 in chapter 2, "Kundalini and Yoga"). *Khechari mudra* (*khe* - ether, *chari* - moving) enhances the upward flow of energy, enabling the yogi to stay in the Brahma Randhra or Shunya Mandala (void center), the hollow space between the twin hemispheres known as the tenth gate of the body, also located within the Sahasrara Chakra.

One who stops the downward flow of nectar becomes immortal in the physical body. He or she gains victory over disease, decay, and death and is able to stop the process of aging, thus remaining ever young, full of vitality and stamina. He or she enjoys eternal bliss through the union of Shiva and Shakti, the ultimate goal of Kundalini Yoga.

Behavioral Characteristics: Crossing the Soma Chakra takes the yogi beyond worldly desires and gives him or her authority over the elements *(tattvatit)*. Then whatever he or she wants happens. Soma Chakra is the place where anxieties and anger subside. Soma is connected with the moon and makes the yogi very peaceful, self-contented, calm, and cool. Bliss is cool.

Soma
Chakra

145

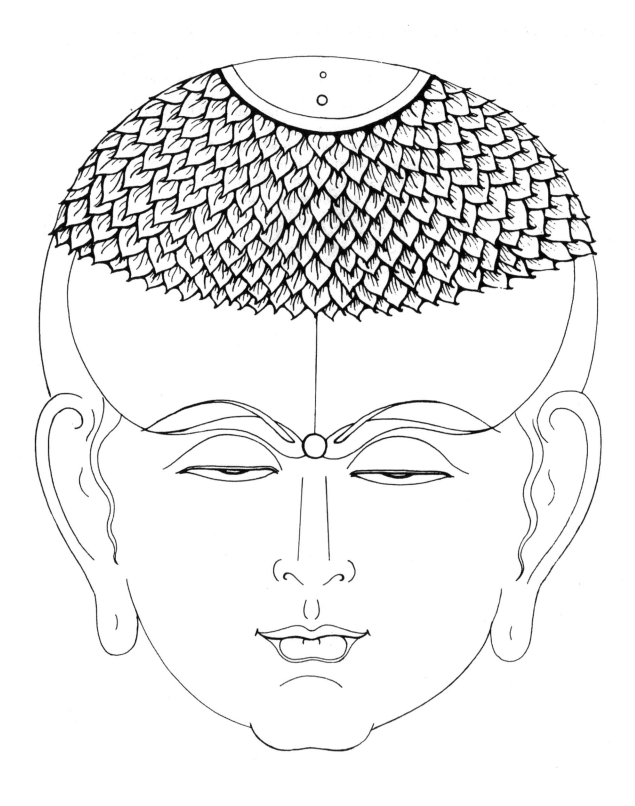

Sahasrara Chakra

सहस्रार चक्र

SAHASRARA CHAKRA
(SEVENTH CHAKRA)

Names:	Sahasrara, Shunya, Niralambapuri
Meanings of the Names:	Thousand-petaled, Void, Dwelling Place Without Support (*niralamba* - without support, *puri* - dwelling place)
Location:	Top of the cranium, cerebral plexus
Seed Sound *(Bija Mantra):*	*Visarga* (a particular breathing sound in the pronunciation of Sanskrit)
Color of the Seed Sound:	Gold
Carrier *(Vahana)* of the Seed Sound:	The motion of *bindu,* the dot above the crescent
Number of Petals:	One thousand
Color of the Petals:	Variegated colors of the rainbow
Seed Sounds of the Petals:	All pure sounds from *AH* to *KSHA,* including all the vowels and consonants of the Sanskrit language
Plane *(Loka):*	Truth, Reality *(Satyam Loka)*
Ruling Planet:	Ketu

Yantra **Form:** Circle as a full moon. In some scriptures the *yantra* is mentioned as *purna chandra (purna* - full, *chandra* - moon), in others as *nirakara* (formless). Above the sphere is an umbrella of one thousand lotus petals arranged in the variegated colors of the rainbow.

Deity: The guru within.

Shakti: Chaitanya. Some scriptures indicate Paramatma, and others, Mahashakti.

Techniques and Effects of Meditation: The following planes are realized by the yogi who has attained seventh-chakra consciousness:

- ☙ The plane of radiation *(Tejas Loka). Tejas* is light, fire, or sight in its finest essence. The yogi becomes illuminated like the sun, a bright being, an enlightened master. His or her aura is continually radiant.

147

- ❧ The plane of primal vibrations *(Omkara)*. *AUM* (or *OM*) is the first sound, continuing infinitely. Centering on *AUM* unlocks the vast resources of cosmic knowledge within, which were blocked in the lower chakras. Here the frequency of *AUM* becomes manifest within the yogi.

- ❧ The gaseous plane *(Vayu Loka)*. The yogi obtains supremacy over *prana*, which becomes so subtle *(sukshma)* that all of the prana within the body is said to be thumb-sized *(angushtha matra)*; if one were to put a piece of glass in front of the yogi's nose, no vapors would deposit on it.

- ❧ The plane of positive intellect *(Subuddhi Loka)*. All value judgments or dualistic perceptions are balanced, preventing negative intellect *(durbuddhi)*, the negation of the divine, from arising within the mind.

- ❧ The plane of happiness *(Sukha Loka)*, which arises when a proper balance in body, psyche, and mind is established.

- ❧ The plane of laziness *(Tamas Loka)* may occur when the yogi attains a state of bliss: when he or she goes into a state of *samadhi*, the physical body becomes totally inactive.

Immortality is achieved within the Sahasrara Chakra. Before attaining this chakra the yogi is unable to reach the unconscious-conscious state of blissful illumination called *asamaprajnata samadhi*. Up to the sixth chakra the yogi may enter a trance in which activity or form still remains within the consciousness. In the Sahasrara Chakra the *prana* moves upward and reaches the highest point. The mind establishes itself in the pure void of Shunya Mandala, the space between the two hemispheres. At this time all feelings, emotions, and desires, which are the activities of the mind, are dissolved into their primary cause. In this state there is no activity of the mind and no knower, no knowledge, nothing to be known. Knowledge, knower, and known all become unified and liberated. The yogi is *sat-chit-ananda*, truth-being-bliss, the highest state of existence.

After experiencing the highest state, which is beyond time and space, cause and effect, and, therefore, beyond bondage and liberation, the yogi remains in *samadhi*, the pure bliss of total inactivity. Such a person will continue to survive in the body until all previous karma has been completely burnt out. Then the yogi can leave the body at will and go to the path of no return, merging into the supreme consciousness.

Behavioral Characteristics in the Sahasrara Chakra: When the Kundalini is raised up to the Sahasrara Chakra, the illusion of "individual self" is dissolved. One is one's own real Self. Even if one stays in the physical body, one retains nondual consciousness, enjoying the play of *lila* without becoming troubled by pleasure or pain, honors or humiliations. The yogi becomes realized, one with the cosmic principles within the body that govern the entire universe. The aspirant gains *siddhis* (powers) as progress is made upward through the chakras until Kamadhenu, the wish-fulfilling cow, is encountered within oneself. One who is established in the Sahasrara Chakra has attained many *siddhis* but has transcended the desire to manifest those powers. The yogi is able to transcend the gunas and becomes a realized being known as *gunatita* (beyond *guna*).

According to the scriptures, Sahasrara is the seat of the self-luminous soul or *chitta,* the essence of being. In the person who has attained Sahasrara, *chitta* is like a screen upon which the reflection of the cosmic Self, the divine, is seen. In the presence of the cosmic Self, it is possible for anyone to feel the divine and, indeed, to realize the divinity within oneself.

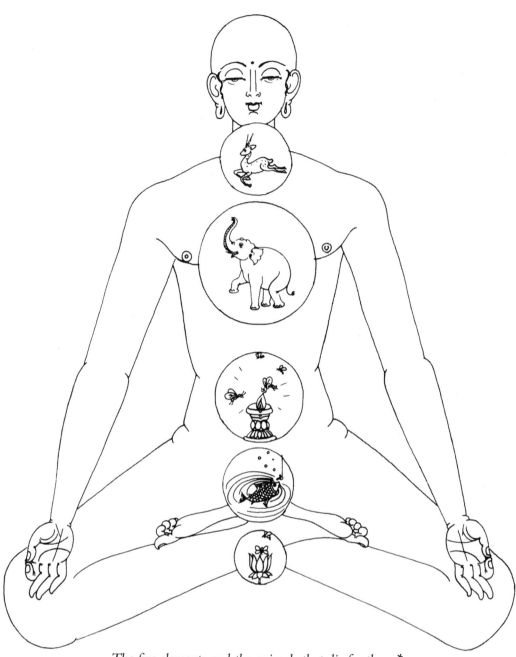

The five elements and the animals that die for them:*

1. Earth – bumblebee dies for smell

2. Water – fish dies for taste

3. Fire – moth dies for sight

4. Air – elephant dies for touch

5. *Akasha* – deer dies for sound

*From the *Vivekachudamani* of Shankaracharya

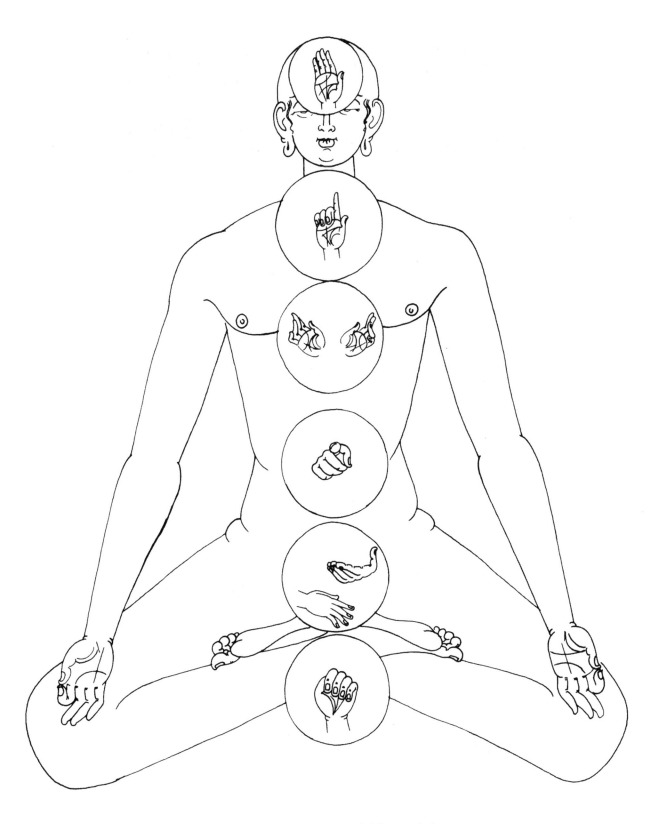

Hand postures (mudras) of different chakras

Chakras, Rebirth, and Spirituality

From God seven *lokas* (that is chakras) have come where the *prana* moves.

Mundakopanishad 2.1.8

Spirituality is the awakening of divinity in consciousness. It is the summum bonum of consciousness in human incarnation, which frees the consciousness from the "mind-body trap." This freedom is obtained by a gradual process of transformation of the sense consciousness of the mind.

It is sense consciousness that perceives the world and that constantly produces uncontrolled thoughts. It desires, feels pleasure and pain, thinks, wills, and—in its pleasure-seeking aspect—sometimes commits excesses.

One can be a great thinker, scientist, artist, or educator without the transformation of sense consciousness. But in experiencing only one aspect of one's being—that which is represented by the I-consciousness surrounded by the sensory world—one remains engaged in the gratification of senses, moving aimlessly with lust and greed in the ocean of *samsara*. By transforming the sense consciousness one can achieve freedom from the slavery of the mind: internal dialogue, uncontrolled thoughts, lust, and greed. Through the transformation of sense consciousness one can experience the other aspect of one's being in which the mind is completely detached from the sensory world and does not think, desire, or will. Then the I-consciousness merges into the supreme consciousness and one moves away from the cycle of birth and death.

152

The I-consciousness engages the mind in continual pleasure-seeking patterns, and these experiences of pleasure develop an affection in the mind for sense consciousness. The mind then wanders around and loses its central focus. The "uncentered" mind is then trapped by the objects of the sensory world, which is a play of the elements *(tattvas)* and the qualities *(gunas)*. An impure mind—or an uncentered mind trapped by desires—leads to bondage. If the purity of the mind is not achieved by the constant practice of concentration aided by mantras, the I-consciousness remains even after one leaves the body. It dwells in different planes *(lokas)*. These planes are directly connected with the human body through the chakras.

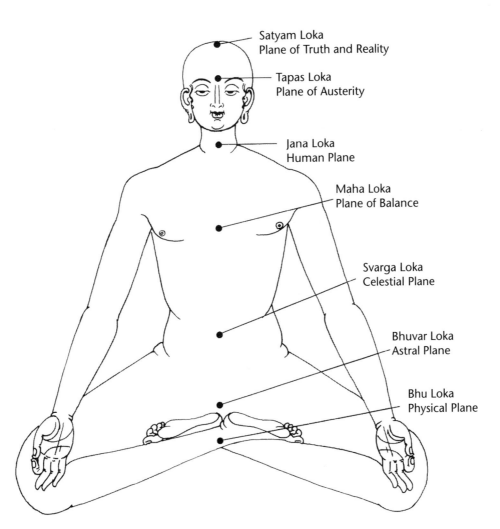

Lokas in the body

As we have seen in the previous chapters, the first five chakras are connected with the five elements—earth, water, fire, air, and *akasha*. The *lokas* connected with those chakras are also connected with their respective elements. The elements belong to the material field and constitute a continuum from the most subtle vibratory level of energy to the most dense. As these elements rise and reign in a fixed succession during the flow of breath through each nostril, the sense consciousness constantly undergoes corresponding changes. All mental and physiological activities, all needs and desires, are connected with these five elements.

The earth element is not the planet Earth. However, the earth element dominates in the planet Earth, known as Bhu (earth) Loka. The seat of both is the Muladhara Chakra. In the human organism, the bones, flesh, skin, Nadis, and hair consist of the earth element. Patience, greed, and the desire for survival are the behavioral attributes connected with the element earth. Its nature is stable. Collecting and saving are the associated activities. When earth dominates for twenty minutes in each breath cycle of sixty minutes, one manifests the desires, activities, nature, and attributes connected with the earth element. If these desires remain unfulfilled, one dwells on the Bhu Loka after death and takes birth again and again as a normal human being.

Similarly, the second chakra, the Svadhishthana Chakra, is the seat of the element water and the astral plane, Bhuvar Loka. Semen, blood, fat, urine, and mucus in the body belong to the water element. Purity and attachment are its attributes, belonging its desire, and peaceful work is the activity of this element. It is cool in nature. In each breath cycle of sixty minutes the element water dominates for sixteen minutes. If the desires of the second chakra are not satisfied, one dwells in the Bhuvar Loka after death. After the period of dwelling in the Bhuvar Loka comes to an end, the person takes birth again on earth to fulfill the desires of the astral plane—as, for example, an artist, musician, dancer, or poet.

The third chakra, the Manipura Chakra, is the seat of the fire element and the celestial plane, Svarga Loka. Hunger, thirst, sleep, lethargy, and personal magnetism *(ojas)* are related to the fire element. Anger is its attribute. Hard labor is the activity of this element. In each breath cycle of sixty minutes this element dominates for twelve minutes. By nature the one dominated by fire is hot-headed and is motivated by the desire for achievement. If one's desires for achievement, such as name, fame, immortality, and power, are not satisfied, one dwells in the Svarga Loka for a period of time after death, by virtue of one's good works *(karmas)* done on earth. After the period of dwelling in Svarga Loka comes to an end, one again takes birth on earth, as a king or administrator of some kind.

The fourth chakra, the Anahata Chakra, is the seat of the element air and the plane of balance, the Maha Loka. Running, hunting, using strength, shrinking (contraction), and growth of the body (expansion) are related to the air element. It creates restlessness, activity, movement, and a desire to do something. Air is responsible for all kinds of movements inside and outside the body, whether circulation of fluids or neuromotor signals in the nervous system. Air is *prana,* energy in the form of the life force that makes one a living and conscious being. In each breath cycle of sixty minutes the air element dominates for eight minutes. If the desires of the fourth chakra are not satisfied in one's life, then after death one dwells in Maha Loka by the virtue of one's good karmas of love, sharing, devotion, selfless service, and compassion done on earth. After the Maha Loka (plane of balance), one again takes birth on earth as a reformer, a saintly person, a devotee, a healer, or a spiritual artist of some kind.

The fifth chakra, the Vishuddha Chakra, is the seat of the element *akasha* and the Jana Loka. Love, enmity, shyness, fear, and attachment are related to the *akasha* element. Its attribute is ego or I-consciousness, its desire is solitude, its activity is thoughts and ideas. In each breath cycle of sixty minutes this element dominates for four minutes. If the desires of the fifth chakra are not fulfilled in one's lifetime, then after death one dwells in Jana Loka (human plane) for a period of time earned through good karmas done during one's life. After Jana Loka the person again takes birth on the planet Earth, as a teacher, a sage, or an interpreter of holy scriptures.

When one goes beyond the elements through the practice of Yoga, one reaches the Ajna Chakra and the plane of austerity, Tapas Loka. One purifies the mind through austerity and, through the transformation of sense consciousness, experiences the higher aspect of one's being. One becomes non-acquisitive, clean, content, and a neutral observer of life and its psychodrama. Mercy, honesty, forgiveness, and firmness enrich this person's life and he or she experiences a splendorous, divine inner force that removes the burden of body consciousness. One achieves full control over one's breath and mind, yet can take another birth if the task of self-realization—which is the merging of I-consciousness into supreme consciousness—has not yet been accomplished. Such a person is reborn as an ascetic, a yogi, an avatar, a bodhisattva, or a prophet. He or she has gone beyond the elements but still must go beyond the *gunas,* and this is only possible through the practice of awakening Kundalini.

A person can function with the body's chemical, mechanical, and electrical energy, and the mind's sense consciousness, without awakening the spiritual energy of Kundalini. However, objective images will always bind the consciousness, and I-consciousness will bring one back to the cycle of life and death. All beings are subject to the law of karma. Good karmas lead to good worlds *(lokas)* and bad karmas to underworlds *(narakas).* These *narakas* are connected with seven chakras below the Muladhara Chakra, which have not been discussed in this book. Kundalini is the spiritual energy that lies dormant in the Muladhara Chakra. It is the energy that supports life and consciousness while remaining coiled, but when it is awakened it brings spiritualized super-consciousness. The sense-mind is transformed into pure mind, which is absorbed by the stream of consciousness flowing in the form of Kundalini Shakti. The mind goes beyond all contraries and realizes the pure being, the changeless, and the only truth *(satya)* in the form of *nirvikalpa samadhi.* This is the plane of Satyam Loka, associated with the Sahasrara Chakra.

After reaching the Sahasrara Chakra and uniting with her counterpart, Shiva, Kundalini remains in union for some time; she then descends to the Muladhara Chakra and coils up again. During this process of descent, the powers of the chakras and of the deities residing in them are restored. Even though Kundalini returns to the Muladhara Chakra and life continues in the body until one's karmas are exhausted, the person now lives in an expanded state of consciousness. He or she lives as a changed person and achieves *nirvana* upon leaving the body.

The body thus purified by Yoga does not decay or decompose easily, like the body of one who is clinging to the material world and the desires for worldly pleasure connected with the lower planes. Those who wish to study more about the planes mentioned in the different chakras are directed to my book *Leela,*[1] which is based on the "game" of knowledge. Additional aspects of the chakras are discussed in my books *Tools for Tantra*[2] and *Breath, Mind, and Consciousness.*[3]

---

1. *Leela: The Game of Self-Knowledge* (Rochester, Vt.: Destiny Books, 1993).
2. *Tools for Tantra* (Rochester, Vt.: Destiny Books, 1986).
3. *Breath, Mind, and Consciousness* (Rochester, Vt.: Destiny Books, 1989).

Appendix

EXTRACTS FROM HINDU SCRIPTURES ON THE VARIOUS STAGES OF YOGA

YOGA

The state of real absorption of consciousness, which is beyond all knowledge, is Yoga. (*Akshyopanishad* 2.3)

Yoga brings a state of deep concentration. (*Shardatilaka* 25.1)

A yogi attains Yoga only in superconcentration. (*Rudrayamalatantra,* part 2, 27.43)

By developing equanimity of the mind, getting beyond all contraries of the world and of the body-consciousness, one is able to realize the one that is pure being, changeless, beyond mind and speech, and the only truth in the transitory world of mind-power-matter. That *brahman* is realized directly in Yoga in the form of *nirvikalpa samadhi.* (*Mahanirvanatantra* 3, 7–8)

Yoga is the control of the *vritties* (mental modifications). (*Shandilyopanishad* 1.7.24)

ASANA (POSTURE)

The body should be trained to be in a state of motionlessness for a prolonged time without discomfort or pain. (*Nadabindu Upanishad* 3.3.1)

In *samadhi* all senses cease to function and the body remains motionless like a piece of wood. (*Nadabindu Upanishad* 3.3.2)

The three worlds are conquered by him who has mastered posture. (*Trishikhi-brahmanopanishad,* mantra section 52)

For purification of the body and for attaining success in Yoga, posture is absolutely necessary. (*Rudrayamalatantra,* part 2.24, 38–39)

Posture helps to make the mind calm. (*Tantrarajatantra* 27, 59)

By the practice of posture the body becomes disease-free, firm, and efficient. (*Grahayamalatantra,* ch. 2)

Physical movements *(mudras)* are not helpful in themselves, nor does concentration alone bring success. One who combines concentration with physical control achieves success and becomes immortal. (*Ishopanishad* 9 and 11)

The yogi should use his body as the lower piece of wood and *pranava (AUM)* the upper piece of wood, and strike them against each other until the fire of realization kindles and he realizes the supreme being. (*Shvetashvataropanishad* 1.14)

When the yogi attains a body purified by Yoga-fire he becomes free from decay and disease, his youth is prolonged, and he lives long. He then experiences superior smell, taste, sight, touch, and sound. (*Shvetashvataropanishad* 2.12)

Asana, when mastered, can destroy all diseases and can even assimilate poisons. If it is not possible to master all *asanas,* master only one and be comfortable with it. (*Shandilyopanishad* 1.3.12–13)

PRANAYAMA (BREATH CONTROL)

There are two causes that make the mind wander around: (1) *Vasanas*—desires that are produced by the latent impressions of feelings—and (2) breathing. If one is controlled the other automatically gets controlled. Of these two, breath should be controlled first. (*Yogakundalyupanishad* 1.1–2)

The breathing process creates images in the mind. When breath becomes calm the mind also becomes calm. (*Yogakundalyupanishad* 89)

The control of breath causes both physical and mental development. (*Varahaupanishad* 5.46–49)

When the Nadis are purified by *nadishodhana pranayama* the *prana* enters the Sushumna with a force and the mind becomes calm. (*Shandilyopanishad* 1.7.9.10)

Assume first a Yoga posture (*asana*); keep the body erect, let the eyes be fixed and jaws relaxed so that the upper teeth do not touch the lower teeth. Turn back the tongue. Use the chin lock (*jalandhara bandha*) and your right hand to breathe through any nostril at will; keep the body motionless and mind at ease. Then practice *pranayama*. (*Trishikhibrahmanopanishad*, mantra section 92–94)

First exhale the air from the lungs through the right nostril by closing the left nostril with the fingers of the right hand. Then inhale through the left nostril counting 16, suspend the breath counting 64, exhale through the right nostril counting 32. (*Trishikhibrahmanopanishad*, mantra section 95–98)

Ten forms of *prana* are controlled by *Pranayama*: (1) *Prana*, (2) *Apana*, (3) *Samana*, (4) *Vyana*, (5) *Udana*, (6) *Kurma*, (7) *Krikila*, (8) *Naga*, (9) *Dhananjaya*, and (10) *Deva Dutta*. (*Mundamalatantra*, ch. 2)

By *pranayama* the throbbing of the *prana* is controlled and the mind becomes calm. (*Gandharvatantra*)

By *pranayama* the internal impurities are removed. It is the best Yoga practice. Without its help liberation is not possible. (*Gandharvatantra*, ch. 10)

By *pranayama* the mind and the senses are purified. (*Kularnavatantra*, ch. 15)

One who is healthy, eats moderately, and can control the breath becomes a yogi. . . . He who is clean and practices sexual control is able to control breath. Regular practice is absolutely necessary. Yoga is not possible without *pranayama*. (*Rudrayamalatantra,* part 2.17.40–43)

In the first stage of *pranayama* perspiration occurs, in the second stage the body shakes, in the highest or third stage the body levitates. *Pranayama* should be practiced regularly until the third stage is reached. (*Shardatilaka* 25.21–22)

When breath control is perfected, the body becomes light, countenance becomes cheerful, eyes become bright, digestive power increases, and it brings internal purification and joy. (*Grahayamalatantra*, ch. 13)

PRATYAHARA (WITHDRAWAL)

The senses and the work organs should be withdrawn into the *manas* (sensemind) and the *manas* should be absorbed into the *jnanatman* (consciousness). (*Kathopanishad* 1.3.13)

The senses should be controlled by will inside the *hrit* (eight-petaled lotus inside the heart chakra, the *Ananda Kanda* or spiritual heart). (*Shvetashvataropanishad* 2.8)

By the concentrated mind the senses should be controlled at their root— in the chakras. (*Trishikhibrahmanopanishad,* mantra section 115)

The mind should be withdrawn by concentrating on the eighteen *adharas* (vital points), one after another, in the following order, while practicing *kumbhaka* (breath suspension): (1) big toe, (2) ankle, (3) calf, (4) knee, (5) thigh, (6) anus, (7) genitals, (8) abdominal region, (9) navel, (10) heart, (11) wrist, (12) elbow, (13) neck, (14) tip of the nose, (15) eyes, (16) roof of the palate, (17) space between the eyebrows, and (18) forehead. The withdrawal of the senses *(indriya aharona)* from the object by applying the power of control (will) is called *pratyahara*. (*Darshanopanishad* 7.1-2)

Breath should be suspended with concentration applied to the following points in succession: (1) roots of the teeth, (2) neck, (3) chest, (4) navel, (5) base of the spine (the region of Kundalini), (6) Muladhara (coccygeal region), (7) hip, (8) thigh, (9) knee, (10) leg, and (11) big toe. This is called *pratyahara* by the ancient yogis. (*Darshanopanishad* 7.5-9)

The control of mind in respect to sensory objects is *pratyahara*. (*Mandalabrahmanopanishad* 1.7)

The withdrawal of the senses from their respective objects toward which they are naturally attracted is called *pratyahara*. (*Yogalattusopanishad* 68.69)

Pratyahara is withdrawal of the senses from their objects, regarding sensory images as God, abandoning the fruits of actions, turning away from all objects, and holding attention in concentration on the eighteen *adharas* in the following succession in ascending and descending order: (1) foot, (2) big toe, (3) ankle, (4) leg, (5) knee, (6) thigh, (7) anus, (8) genitals, (9) navel, (10) heart, (11) neck, (12) larynx, (13) palate, (14) nostrils, (15) eyes, (16) the space between the eyebrows, (17) forehead, and (18) head. (*Shandilyopanishad* 8.1–2)

Fluctuations in mind are caused by desires; when desires are controlled by *pratyahara*, the mind becomes still and concentrates on God. (*Rudrayamalatantra*, part 2, 24.137)

The mind connected with senses and their objects is irresistible, firm, difficult to control, and unwilling to obey; the withdrawal of it by the power of will is called *pratyahara*. By practice of *pratyahara* the yogi becomes calm and is able to concentrate deeply. This leads him to Yoga. (*Rudrayamalatantra,* part 2, 27.28–30)

In *kumbhaka* (suspension of breath) the mind should be concentrated; beginning from Muladhara to other chakras step-by-step—this is called *pratyahara*. (*Tantrarajatantra* 27, 70)

DHARANA (CONCENTRATION)

Dharana is holding the divine spirit in consciousness during concentration. (*Amritanadopanishad* 15)

The withdrawal of consciousness from the perceptive field and holding it in the super-conscious field is *dharana*. (*Mandalabrahmanopanishad* 1.1.8)

A practitioner of Yoga after practicing *yama, niyama, asana,* and *pranayama* should hold his mind on the five forms of elements in their respective centers within the body. This is called *dharana*. (*Trishikhibrahmanopanishad,* mantra section 133–134)

Dharana is of three kinds:
1. Holding concentration on the divine aspect of the self.
2. Holding concentration on *akasha* (void) in the *hrit* center (the spiritual heart inside the Anahata Chakra with an eight-petaled lotus).
3. Holding concentration on the five divine forms: (1) Brahma, (2) Vishnu, (3) Braddha Rudra, (4) Ishana Shiva, and (5) Panchavaktra Shiva. (*Shandilyopanishad* 1.9.1)

Whatever is seen with the eyes, heard with the ears, smelled with the nose, tasted with the tongue, and touched by the skin should be regarded as divine being. In this manner the object of the senses should be transformed into divine being and held in consciousness. (*Yogatattvopanishad* 69–72)

Concentration on the big toe, ankle, knee, scrotum, genitals, navel, heart, neck, throat, uvula, nose, space between the eyebrows, breast, and head in *kumbhaka* (breath suspension) is called *dharana*. (*Gandharvatantra,* ch. 5)

The holding in consciousness of certain vital points while holding the breath is called *dharana*. (*Prapanchasaratantra* 19, 21–22)

Concentration on the six subtle centers and Kundalini (the coiled power) is termed *dharana*. (*Rudrayamalatantra,* part 2, 27, 34–35)

Concentration on the whole divine form is *dhyana* (meditation) while concentration only on one point at a time is *dharana*. (*Bhutashuddhitantra*, ch. 9)

DHYANA (MEDITATION)

Eyes cannot see the supreme being nor can words express it—nor can it be reached by other senses and cognitive faculties. The supreme being is only revealed in *dhyana*. *Dhyana* (true meditation) is only possible when consciousness is spiritualized by purity of knowledge of the self. (*Mundakopanishad* 8.1.8)

Dhyana is concentration on the divine being, who is quiescent, luminous, pure, and blissful in the *hrit* center (spiritual heart). (*Kaivalyopanishad* 5)

Concentration on the universal form of God, realized by concentration on mantra, and then concentrating on God without form is *dhyana*. (*Darshanopanishad* 9.1-2-3-5)

When concentration reaches the phase of nondual consciousness (seeing the supreme being abiding in each and every particle), that is *dhyana*. (*Mandalabrahmanopanishad* 1.1.9)

Dhyana is of two types: (1) *saguna dhyana*, meditation on God with form and attributes, and (2) *nirguna dhyana*, meditation on God without form and attributes. Doing breath suspension and meditation on the deity is *saguna dhyana,* and meditation on the supreme being without form is *nirguna dhyana. Nirguna dhyana* leads to *samadhi*. (*Yogatattvopanishad* 105)

Dhyana is to hold the form of the deity in the consciousness without interruption. (*Prapanchasaratantra* 19.22–23)

Dhyana is concentration on the form of the deity of the mantra. (*Kularnavatantra*, ch. 17)

SAMADHI
(SUPER-CONSCIOUSNESS)

The state in which consciousness is in concentration and is illuminated by the divine light—without any desire—that super-conscious state is called *samadhi*. (*Annapurnopanishad* 1.48)

By sensory control, control of desires, concentration, and asceticism a yogi will be in *samadhi*. In *samadhi* all love is directed toward the supreme being; one is fully attached and absorbed in Him and experiences all bliss in Him. From *samadhi,* knowledge contained in the word-form *(pranava)* is revealed to the yogi. (*Nrisinghalapinyopanishad* 2.6.4)

The continuous flow of consciousness in the form of the *brahman,* the supreme being in which the I-ness has been dissolved, is called *samprajnata samadhi.* It is attained by prolonged practice of *dhyana.* (*Muktikopanishad* 2.53)

The mind operating at the sensory level is the root cause of all worldly knowledge. If the mind is dissolved, there will be no worldly knowledge. Therefore, keep the consciousness fixed on the supreme being in deepest concentration. (*Adhyatmopanishad* 26)

Samadhi is that state in which consciousness is only in the nature of the object concentrated on and is still, like the flame of a lamp in a windless place, and from which the feeling of the action of concentration and I-ness ("I am concentrating") has gradually disappeared. (*Adhyatmopanishad* 35)

That state in which the mind is devoid of restlessness, I-ness, pleasure, pains, and in which consciousness is absolutely motionless like a rock, in deepest concentration, is *samadhi.* The state in which there is tranquillity is *samadhi.* (*Annapurnopanishad* 1.49–50)

That state of consciousness in which there are no objects, no passions, no aversions, but there is supreme happiness and superior power, is *samadhi*. (*Mahopanishad* 4.62)

When consciousness reaches a state in which it becomes uniform (nondual) it is *samadhi*. (*Amritanadopanishad* 16)

Samadhi is that state in which the consciousness is in deepest concentration and awareness becomes united with supreme consciousness. (*Darshanopanishad* 10.1)

Samadhi is that in which the I-consciousness *(ekata)* merges in supreme consciousness. *(Gandharvatantra,* ch. 5)

As a crystal of salt thrown into water dissolves in water and becomes one with water, so the state in which unity in I-consciousness and supreme consciousness is achieved is called *samadhi*. (*Saubhagyalakshmi Upanishad* 2.14)

Samadhi is that state in which I-consciousness and supreme consciousness become one. It is without duality and full of bliss, and therein remains only supreme consciousness. (*Shandilyopanishad* 1.11.1)

When concentrative consciousness is lost it is *samadhi*. (*Mandalabrahmanopanishad* 1.1.10)

When the uniform concentrative consciousness is dissolved by the most intensified concentration, there remains only the being of supreme consciousness. (*Annapurnopanishad* 1.23)

When the deepest concentration on the supreme *brahman* also disappears by itself within, there arises *nirvikalpa samadhi*—in which all latent impressions of feelings are eliminated. (*Annapurnopanishad* 4.62)

GLOSSARY

adi shakti – primal or supreme power

ahamkara – I-consciousness, ego

akasha – void, also space

amrita – immortal nectar

anahata nada or *shabda brahma* –
the unstruck cosmic sound

ananda – bliss

anna – food

apana – one of the five main *pranas*

artha – security, meaning

asamaprajnata samadhi – unconscious-
conscious state, blissful illumination,
supreme consciousness

asana – posture

bhakti – divine love, devotion

bhoga – enjoyment

bija mantras – seed sounds

bindu – semen, physical male seed,
the supreme truth that is the seed
of all manifest phenomena

bodhisattva – compassionate, concern
for others' welfare

buddhi – intellect

chit – truth

chitta – being, feeling self

damaru – drum

devata – divine form

dharma – code of conduct

dhyana – meditation

doshas – humors

gandha – smell

gunas – qualities

homa(m) – fire ceremony

hrit – heart

indriyas – sense organs and work organs

jada – non-sentience

japa – repetition

jiva – the individual or individuated self

kama – enjoyment

kevali kumbhaka – automatic breath
suspension

khechari mudra – dwelling in the space
between the eyebrows

kosha – sheath

kshata chakra bhedana – piercing the six
chakras

kshata karmas – six acts of purification

kumbhaka – breath suspension

lila – sport, play, game

lingam – male generative organ

loka – plane

mahabhutas – gross elements

manas – mind

manovahi nadis – channels of the
mind, channels that carry mental
energy

mantra – sound that enables a state of
concentration, free from worldly
thoughts

mantra japa – mantra repetition

matrikas – sound units, letters of the
alphabet

maya – the veiling power; the ever-
changing illusory existence, the
phenomenon

meru danda – spinal column

moksha – liberation

mudra – a specific kind of muscular
control practice to aid meditation

nada – pure cosmic sound

nada-bindu – the primal sound vibration from which the universe unfolded; the crescent *(nada)* with a dot *(bindu)*

nadis – carriers of subtle energy in the body

nirguna – without attributes

ojas – personal magnetism, radiance

padarthas – four objects of achievement

param shiva – supreme consciousness

prakriti – primordial nature, equipoised state of the three gunas

prana – vital life force

pranava – AUM

pranayama – conscious breath control

pranavahi nadis – channels of *prana*, channels that carry pranic energy

pratyahara – withdrawal of sensory perceptions

rajas, rajasik – passion, activity, mobility

rasa – taste

rasas – moods

rishi – seer or saint

rupa – form, fire

sadhaka – aspirant

sadhana – practice

saguna – with attributes

samadhi – realized nonduality, complete equilibrium

samprajnata samadhi – super-conscious concentration

sat – truth

sattva, sattvik – equanimity, lightness, purity

shabda – sound

shakti – energized consciousness

shastras – scriptures

shuddha vidya – pure knowledge

siddhasana – accomplished posture

siddhis – powers, accomplishments, attainments

soma – nectar

sparsha – touch

tamas, tamasik – sloth, inertia, darkness

tanmatra – only that, principle

tanmatras – pure essences, principles, pure frequencies

tantra – expanded consciousness

tapasya – austerity or penance

tattva – element

tattvas – eternal verities

turiya – fourth state of consciousness, nondual, transcendental consciousness

vahana – carrier, vehicle

vayu – air

vedic – of the Veda, of the sacred teachings

vidya – knowledge

vritties – mental modifications, qualities

yantra – shape, form, pattern

yoga – to unite, to join, detachment

yogi – practitioner of yoga, yoga adept

yoni – female generative organ

INDEX

An "f" following a page number indicates that information is found in a figure.